Herefordshire's Home Front in the First World War

Herefordshire's Home Front in the First World War

by

Bill Laws

Logaston Press

LOGASTON PRESS
Little Logaston Woonton Almeley
Herefordshire HR3 6QH
logastonpress.co.uk

First published by Logaston Press 2016
Copyright © Bill Laws 2016

ISBN 978 1 910839 06 5

Typeset by Logaston Press
and printed and bound in Poland by
www.lfbookservices.co.uk

CONTENTS

ACKNOWLEDGEMENTS

Herefordshire's Home Front in the First World War is a collaborative project between Logaston Press, Herefordshire Libraries, Herefordshire Museum Service and the Herefordshire Archive and Record Centre. The book is based on material held by these agencies, personal recollections and stories gleaned from the local press of the day.

The author is indebted to the library, museum and archive staff and to Herefordshire Council's Sarah Chedzoy. Thanks are also due to Sandy Green for proof reading; Andy Johnson for editing; Jeanette Bates; the Bellamy family, Kings Caple; the late Derrick Blake; Michael Bolt; Rolly Bradstock; Angus and Regina Brymer; Glen and Margaret Butcher; David and Margaret Clarke and Fownhope History Group; Don and Pat Davies; Stuart Dove; Faith Ford, Judith Morgan and Bartonsham History Group (www.bartonshamhistory.org.uk); Stan and Mary Fryer; Nicola Goodwin and BBC Hereford and Worcester; Michael Griffith; John and Anne Harrison; Eileen Klotz, Bobbie Blackwell and Herefordshire Lore; Jonathan Hopkinson and Leintwardine History Society; Mark Hubbard; Elinor Kelly, Norman Richardson and the Peace Pledge Union; Keith and Krystyna James; Marsha O'Mahoney and the Ross Gazette; Fiona Penwarne and Sara Tait; Dave Newell, The Village Quire and Leominster Museum; Barbara Perrin and Elizabeth Patrick; Liz Pitman; Pete Redding; Winnie Reece; Reg and Joyce Robins; Jerry Ross and David Lovelace; Ivy Manning; Paul Selfe and Eardisland Heritage and History Group; Anne Spurgeon; Tim Smith; Joan Thomas; Julie Orton-Davies and the WEA; Colonel Andy Taylor; Sue Verrill; and Bill Webb.

Thanks too to Peggy for her curiosity and Abby for her patience.

A note on Imperial to Metric conversions

Quantities and spellings are taken as published in the local press at the time.

Currency
1/-, 1s (one shilling): in 1970 when decimalisation was introduced a shilling was valued at five new pence (5p). Twelve old pence (12d) made a shilling and 20 shillings made £1. The average annual wage of a labourer in 1914 was £106.

Weight
1lb (pound) = 0.454 kg
1cwt hundredweight = 112lbs or 50.8 kg

Land measures
1 acre = 4,046.86 square metres (or 0.404686 hectares)

Chapter 1

1913

In 1913 Hereford's soldiers enjoyed an almost idyllic existence with good pay, holidays and the opportunity to travel to Ireland and India, wrote a reporter in the *Hereford Times*. The newspaper offered no hint of the terrible days to come.

One night that summer, a year before the opening salvo of the Great War, Eardisley residents were startled by the sound of gunfire. The following morning the rector, the Revd S. Montgomery Campbell, summoned PC Brown to apprehend the careless poacher, if such it was, for recklessly disturbing the peace.

Aside from the excitement at Eardisley, Herefordshire life carried on much as before. Councillors in Peterchurch were campaigning for action over a dangerous bend called Cheshyre's Turn ('Someone will be killed,' warned Councillor Ballard); Albert Marriott was advertising his new Alldays Midget car, price £130, at the Motor House, St Owen Street, Hereford, and Herefordshire Council's Agricultural Committee was debating the 30 shillings compensation then on offer 'for the destruction of tuberculous cattle'.

At Whitchurch the sub-postmaster's sons, Walter and Vivian Banchini, were meeting their friends, Harold, Wilfred and Leonard Redler, the sons of the Congregational minister, outside the post office. Sixteen miles away at Breinton Court, Captain Gerald Lea was admiring a portrait of his new wife, Brenda, painted by a promising young artist, Brian Hatton. Hatton, meanwhile, was making the most of his long summer holiday sketching the shire horses and waggoners on James Powell's farm at Warham Court in Breinton. The waggoners themselves and hard-working men like tenant farmer Alfred James of Marsh Farm, Upton Bishop took their holidays, like the banks, on just six days in the year.

At the other end of the social spectrum were families such as the Cawleys at Berrington Hall near Leominster where Harold had recently celebrated his 35th birthday with brothers John and Oswald. Another fine country seat was Holme Lacy House, the country retreat of the Australian brewing empire and its privileged sons, Douglas, Selwyn and Archibald Lucas-Tooth.

The coming war would slaughter them all, the Banchinis and the Redlers, Captain Lea and Brian Hatton, the Cawleys and the Lucas-Tooths – bar one. Only Alfred James survived, grieving for his friends, comrades and the estimated 3,000 Herefordshire dead,

A postcard of the Territorial Army church parade along Broad Street in 1909.
The life of the soldier was far preferable to the hard life of the farm labourer,
suggested a *Hereford Times* reporter. (Photo: Dorothy Jancey)

most of them young, unmarried lads who had the misfortune to be in their late teens and twenties in 1913.

The approaching conflict would impact on the lives of every one of Herefordshire's 114,000 people. War would alter the look of the countryside: ancient woodlands and venerable old trees were axed to feed the insatiable demand for timber required in the trenches in France and traditional swards were put to the plough to service the needs of the armies. Herefordshire sacrificed more of its traditional milk meadows to the new tractor ploughs than any other county in England or Wales. In the process the county failed its children, emptying classrooms so that its scholars could work the farms. By the end of the war Herefordshire would have the worst record for school attendance in the country.

In 1913, almost half the population lived in country communities, places such as the picture-book village of Eardisland. Here tenant farmers drove the local economy under the benign eye of the squire and Boer War veteran, Colonel Peter Clowes. Clowes, his wife Edith and their only son Warren or 'Pat' (he would be killed in March 1918) occupied Burton Court and exerted a significant influence on the community. Tenants' homes, painted in the estate colours, were promptly vacated when the worker died; children received time off from school for the Clowes family's shooting parties; villagers doffed their caps or curtsied when the Clowes passed by. (A village teenager was summoned for a ticking off by Mrs Clowes after being spotted 'walking out' with one of her servants.) Col Clowes set up the village cricket club and Scout troop while Mrs Clowes sat on the magistrates' bench, the Weobley Workhouse Board of Guardians, rural council, county wages committee and local hunt.

The Breinton Court family scrapbook captured the pre-war pleasures of the traditional New Year's house party. Four years before the war Henry and Jessie Wadworth pose for their photograph at Breinton Court with guests including Christabel Bourne and her husband-to-be Edward Hopton (above). Ten days later it was the turn of the Hoptons at Homend, Stretton Grandison (below). Both Edward and Guy Hopton would be killed in the ensuing war.
(Photos: Hereford Records and Archive Centre)

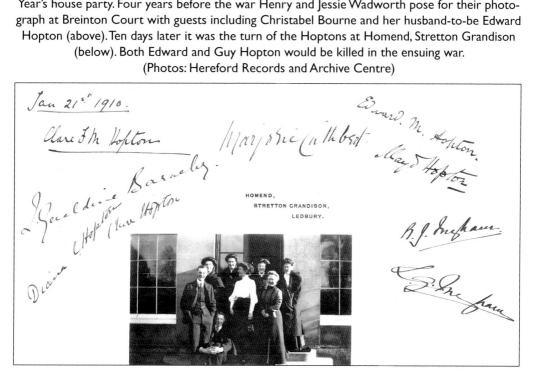

The prospects of social change did not appeal to middle and upper class families such as the Clowes of Burton Court. But the war brought radical change to Herefordshire families. (Photo: Eardisland Heritage & History Group)

Families like these generated considerable local income. Percy Pritchard lived above the family's tailor shop in High Town, Hereford. In 1913 he had just turned 17. 'There was a big livery trade. The county families had their coachmen, footmen, butler and they'd have two outfits a year, all hand made, box coats with crested buttons for the coachmen. The clergy [was] a big trade too and every farmer was a riding man [who required] his britches and riding jacket. Then there was the hunting trade and all the huntsmen's uniforms.'

It made work for men like Stanley Powell, a jobbing tailor who lodged at 16A Widemarsh Street. Stanley was a committed socialist and pacifist, a man who believed passionately in social change. The two tailors, Percy and Stanley, lived only a few doors away from each other, but their lives were destined to take very different paths: while Percy came close to death on the frozen shores of Gallipoli, Stanley would end the war a fugitive after being sentenced to two years' hard labour for refusing to fight.

Socialism was anathema to most people living in what was a deeply conservative county. When Bromyard's new vicar, Revd Francis Howard Powell, stepped into the pulpit to deliver his first sermon, 11 members of the congregation stormed out in protest having unsuccessfully petitioned the bishop against Powell and what they regarded as his progressive theological views. The county was politically conservative too. Leominster's 1912 by-election had seen old Etonian and Conservative Captain Henry Fitzherbert Wright take over from Sir James Rankin of Bryngwyn Manor, Wormelow and sent to parliament. Hereford had voted in Liberal Unionist William Hewins, the former (and the first) head of the London School of Economics, while Ross was represented by another Conservative and Old Etonian, Captain Percy Archer Clive of Perrystone

Court. Hewins, Wright and Clive would represent Herefordshire until 1918, Hewins and Wright stepping down while Clive, by then a distinguished military hero, would die on the Western Front.

Addressing a Unionist fête at Whitecross that summer, MP William Hewins expressed a commonly held view when he declared: 'The foundations of your Europe [were] not laid by a lot of Radicals and Socialists [there were cries of 'hear hear']. They were laid by people who believed in the masses of the people, who were loyal to the people, and who thought that England was worth something, and had some lesson to teach the races of the world [applause].' There was little in his speech to suggest this was a nation heading for war, like a ship with a dysfunctional captain at the helm. Nor was there anything to suggest that class, paternalism and sexism would be challenged in the days ahead. Yet they would: in five years' time working women would be holding their own in most field and factory jobs while a former child farm labourer would astonish the county set by standing as a Labour candidate against the ruling Conservative MP.

At the year's end a *Hereford Times* reporter visited Copthorne Barracks in Shrewsbury, the home of the King's Shropshire Light Infantry (KSLI) to see for himself the 'raw material made for defeating the King's enemies in the field of battle'. He did not identify who these 'enemies' might be, but assured his readers that here were men who, once trained, would pass into the Army Reserve and be 'prepared at any moment to return to barracks and take up arms'.

The correspondent revealed that the name Herefordshire would shortly be added to that of the King's Shropshires since 'men from this county are proud to belong to it and are joining the colours every week'. (The regimental name never did change, much to the annoyance of Herefordshire's recruiting officers.)

Seeking to dispel the notion 'that barrack life is one long monotonous routine for turning out soldiers in the approved pattern', the article revealed the main preoccupations of a Herefordshire soldier in 1913: Ireland and India. 'The men intended for the line battalions are, at the end of their first period of training viz three months, drafted into the 1st Battalion of the KSLI at Tipperary.' They were subsequently drafted into the 2nd Battalion stationed in India, shortly to be commanded by Major Bridgford who was then leaving for Secunderabad.

In the Special Reserve, for which the raw recruits trained initially, the men were drilled every day except Sundays: marching, wheeling and doubling at 'the insistent voice of the drill sergeant' before dinner at 1pm followed by more drilling, elementary evening school and what the reporter described as a substantial tea. Evenings offered rest and recuperation in the gymnasium, over billiards or in the reading room.

Taken with the additional services of the Regimental Aid Society which provided temporary relief to ex-soldiers, 'the life of a soldier [could] seem almost idyllic and certainly preferable', wrote the correspondent, 'to life as a farm hand with its long hours, small pay, and no holidays'. He predicted that life in the barracks would soon attract many more 'strong and sturdy youths' away from the farms.

If they had known the future, most farm boys might have done better to have stayed where they were. In 1913, however, many were prepared to strike over their poor pay and conditions. The Workers' Union, under its leader Sidney Box of 27 Chandos Street,

Hereford, was going head to head with those in charge of the perennial business of raising, milking and butchering beasts, and growing crops and fodder. Labourers were now demanding a half-day holiday on Saturday, fixed hours of work through the week and three months' notice before having to quit the farm cottage. The men also wanted better pay than their current 16 or 17 shillings a week: 4d an hour or £1 a week in summer, 18 shillings in winter with 6d an hour overtime and 'not less than' £1 in harvest money. In the following years, struggling through the mud of Mons or a hail of machine gun fire over Suvla Bay the average labourer turned private would be earning just over one shilling a day.

For now the union had no issue with the traditional labourers' perk, cider, although one Ross farmer blamed the drink on all their problems. 'There are very few good men in our district who receive less than £1 a week cash and kind,' he declared, admitting that he paid only 16 shillings a week, yet promising to 'give them 2s a week more money with pleasure if they would give up their cider'.

'I do not give cider,' declared another farmer, speaking to the press. Described as a prosperous hop farmer, Mr J. Thompson of Tea-Kettle Farm at the Hyde, Woolhope told reporters: 'I pay my best men 16 shillings a week. I have some stockmen who get their house in addition to that, and of course the men have gardens and potato ground.' Sidney Box responded through the letters column of the local newspapers pointing out that the pay of rural workers was well below the national poverty line of £1 6d a week. The injustices facing farm workers was 'appalling' and the tied cottage system represented 'the curse of agriculture'.

Matters finally boiled over the following July on the very eve of war. The union had given one month's notice of a strike as the county's crops sweltered under a heatwave. Lightning had killed two horses at the farm of a Mr Edwards in Whitchurch, two cows on Mr Drinkwater's at Bernithan and a sow on the Kymin. In the heat of the moment, and with six days to go before the start of the strike, a group of Ross farmers warned: 'The harvest will be gathered.' Even the affluent Mr Thompson privately conceded that the farmers would eventually have to raise wages. Another farmer protested that 'if the men had approached their employers, things could have been settled without any fuss or bother', but added ominously: 'The farmers are reasonable, but if once they get their backs up there will be a bad time for the labourers.' In the end the farmhands backed down. Aside from some angry words in the farmyard and a walk out by a few, the harvest went ahead, leaving simmering resentment on both sides. Unresolved, the issue of farm wages would continue to haunt the county's farmers.

The farm labourers were not alone in threatening to withhold their labour during 1913. Throughout the year relations between the county's Education Committee, school governors and staff at the county's 178 schools had deteriorated over the issue of pay. This was a national dispute, but when the Education Committee began replacing striking teachers with strike-backing educators, relations were considerably soured.

Most teachers kept quiet about their political leanings, although many privately supported those actively campaigning for a woman's right to vote. The suffragettes (from *suffrage*, the right to vote) were as active locally as they were nationally. Their leader Emmeline Pankhurst, who had been released 'in a very critical condition' from

The headmaster and mistress of Newton St Margarets photographed by local farmer Richard Jenkins. By 1914 many teachers, unhappy with their pay and conditions, went on strike.
The Education Committee responded by replacing them with teachers from elsewhere. (Photo: Winnie Reece)

VOTES FOR WOMEN.

Photo. by Schmidt, Manchester.

MRS. PANKHURST,
Founder and Hon. Sec., National Women's Social and Political Union, 4, Clement's Inn, Strand, W.C.

Beatrice Parlby of Castle Cliffe, Hereford treasured her signed photo of Emeline Pankhurst. Like her sisters she was a staunch supporter of the suffragette movement. (Photo: Mark Hubbard)

Holloway prison that summer, sent a postcard of support to Beatrice Parlby, who lived at Castle Cliffe on the banks of the Wye in Hereford. Beatrice and her sisters, the daughters of the former manager of the city gas works William Parlby, were staunch suffragettes. They were deeply upset by the death of Emily Davison, killed a month earlier when she was knocked down and trampled by the king's horse at the Epsom Derby. Her death exasperated the vicar of Moorfields, Hereford, Revd E.F. Powell, who felt compelled to write to the *Hereford Times* to say that while he was 'obviously an advocate of votes for women' he questioned 'in what way is a cause commended to human judgement by a woman allowing herself to be trampled upon by a racehorse?'

Undismayed, the women of Herefordshire continued to campaign for the right to vote. It would provoke the vicar of Leominster, the Revd H.G. Burden, to lock his church the following July fearing an attack from this 'vicious body of fanatics'. Vicious or not, they enjoyed considerable local support as a Miss Fraser told a meeting in Colwall held, ironically, in the village workmen's club. Fraser was a member of the local branch of the National Union of Suffragette Societies (NUSS) and she declared that the British movement with 60,000 members would win the vote just as women had in Australia, Norway, Finland, Iceland, Denmark, America and Holland. Leominster's citizens, encouraged perhaps by their vicar, were less sympathetic. When the NUSS's Mrs Cornmeadow and Miss Knight addressed a crowd in Corn Square they were pelted with gooseberries and rotten eggs and were forced to retreat under the protection of the police.

Rescuing suffragettes was but one of the tasks undertaken by the county constabulary which, in 1913, fulfilled its customary role of keeping the peace and bringing felons to justice. These ranged from dealing with unfortunates such as a Bishopston farm labourer, John Bevan, found

FLYING EXHIBITIONS

BY

Mr. B. C. HUCKS,

The Famous British Airman

(On his new 80-h.p. Gnome Bleriot Monoplane which he has just purchased for the sum of £1,200)

AT

THE BARTONSHAM MEADOW, HEREFORD

(By kind permission of his Worship, the Mayor of Hereford)

ON

Wednesday and Thursday, Sept. 3rd & 4th, 1913.

TWO EXHIBITIONS ON EACH DATE.

MR. B. C. HUCKS

WILL GIVE A

SENSATIONAL DISPLAY

INCLUDING

Open Demonstration Flying, Altitude Flying, and Fancy Flying.

Passenger Carrying Exhibitions at arranged times :—

FEE: £5 PER FLIGHT.

Can be seen perfectly only from the Flying Ground.

SPECIAL MOTOR CAR ENCLOSURES.

TIMES OF FLYING—FROM 2-30 P.M. TO 4-30 P.M.; AND FROM 6 P.M. TO DUSK.

Admission to the Ground, 1s. and 6d.

1s. Tickets can be obtained at 9d. each until Sept. 1st,
Public View of the Aeroplane on the Ground.
For Railway arrangements see Companies Bills. 2882

B C HUCKS
166 PICCADILLY
LONDON W

Pioneer pilot Bentfield Hucks gave many Herefordians their first glimpse of an aeroplane in 1913. The aviator went on to test fly fighter planes, but died during the Spanish flu epidemic in November 1918.

helplessly drunk in Hereford city (he was fined 5 shillings) and a butcher's boy, Reg Morris, arrested for beating the sheep he was driving to Hereford Market (fined 5 shillings), to apprehending three Orcop poachers, Henry White, Fred Davies and Jeremiah Castree, who were caught taking game birds. Exemplary prison sentences of up to four months and a spell of hard labour were handed down to them by Judge Sir Thomas Edward Scrutton. There were fighting bulls to deal with in Etnam Street, Leominster and at Hereford Market where Risbury farmer Fred Riley was almost trampled to death by his Hereford bull which had locked horns with a Shorthorn. And there were crowds to control when the famous airman, Bentfield Hucks, the first British aviator to perform a loop in an aircraft, arrived in Hereford that September.

As the city Boy Scouts prepared to rally on Hereford's Castle Green, Mr Hucks offered flights aboard his 80 horsepower, £1,200 Gnome Blériot Monoplane on the Bartonsham Farm meadows. The singular sight of a flying machine drew hundreds to the meadows in spite of an assertion in the *Paris La Controverse*, republished by the *Hereford Times*, that this new aerial science was as out of date as horse-powered transport. The author predicted that, since conventional aeroplanes could not make more than 125mph, they would shortly be replaced by rocket-powered craft. He could not have predicted the approaching surge in military aviation nor its consequences: Bentfield Hucks went on to become a Royal Flying Corps test pilot around the same time that a young Ross soldier, Archie Cole from Dancing Green, lost his right arm when a German airplane dropped a bomb on his position in France. (Several county men would be killed or injured in air attacks in the years ahead.)

For now Bentfield Hucks charged £5 for a flight over the city in his flying machine. There were few takers amongst working people. Average earnings listed in that winter's situations vacant columns ranged from £20 to £25 a year for a children's nurse, lady cook, housekeeper or laundry maid, to 12 shillings a week for a blacksmith, £1 a week for a handyman, 21 shillings for a groom/gardener and, for the better paid bricklayers, 8d an hour.

Railwaymen were, at around 30 shillings a week, relatively well paid. The nation and the county were covered by a railway system that was barely half a century old yet stitched together all of Herefordshire's market towns. In 1913 engineman John Phillips of 34 Ryeland Street, Hereford could still recall driving the first Great Western Railway (GWR) train, with Queen Victoria on board, from Shrewsbury to Hereford 59 years earlier. (There was room for improvement on the railways: Kington farmers who had to load their beasts on the cattle trucks at 6.30 in the morning for the 10.30 Leominster sales were campaigning constantly for a later cattle train.)

Household rents averaged around 3s 1½d a week while land rents, for example on a council smallholding situated on the flat, fertile plain of Rotherwas, stood at between £77 and £131 a year. Wages were rising in the engineering trades, but for other occupations they remained unchanged or even lower than eight years earlier. There was no lack of readers responding to enticing advertisements offering 'splendid openings for the British Orchardist and Dairy Farmer with capital' in Western Australia. Hereford's Holy Trinity parish magazine published an article about Australia, describing life there as 'happy and useful' in contrast to the 'casual labour, loafing about and unemployment' of home. It captured the imagination of many county men including William Charles, a 21-year-old postman from De Lacy Street, Hereford, who by March 1913, had left to work on the cattle stations down under: two years later he would find himself fighting beside his former county friends on the beaches of Gallipoli (see page 56).

The depressed economy meant that roadsters, vagrants, casuals and tramps roaming the country in search of work were a common sight. The number of casuals was considerable: in November 1913 Mr M.J. Swabey, chairman of the Hereford Workhouse, which sheltered 103 men, 57 women, 4 boys and 8 girls, reported an additional 179 vagrants (160 men, 15 women and 4 children) passing through in a single week.

According to Mr W.S. Lane, a member of the Ledbury Workhouse Board of Guardians, most were idle townspeople set on having 'a summer's outing at the expense of the ratepayers'. Late in 1913 and under the chairmanship of Mr W.L. Pritchett, Mr Lane and his fellow Guardians baulked at a government proposal, recently adopted by the Ross Board, to issue casuals with 'way and food tickets'. The proposal was, thought Mr Lane, a step too far for these undesirable people who, he revealed, operated a system of marking gateposts at places considered to be a soft touch. Unlike Board member

Revd A.H. Knapp ('I like tramps calling at my house because it gives me the opportunity to interview them,' he told the Board), Mr Lane and a Mr Riley held that 'these tramping people are worthless'. The meal ticket plan was not adopted. Charitable aid, then and during the ensuing war, often carried the sting of judgement in its tail.

Some causes did meet with general approval. They included the popular Pound Day, which raised funds for Eastnor's Home for Waifs and Strays, and a national campaign to raise £100,000 to send a British sportsmen's team to compete in the 1916 Olympic Games due to be hosted by Germany. (In the event the Games were postponed by war.)

Germany seemed to cast a continual shadow on the Herefordshire horizon. When he spoke to guests at a garden party at Broadlands, Hereford, the home of Judge Harris Lea, Hereford MP William Hewins had to admit 'there has never been as much cause for apprehension in regard to national defence as now'. He shared the platform with Vice Admiral Robert Cuming, who warned landlocked Herefordians that they could not always rely on the great British Navy to protect them from their enemies. Cuming argued that the nation should look more closely at its soldiers in the Territorial Force, a force that was under strength. The force had recently fallen short of its own target by 60,000. He blamed the 'woefully inadequate' attitude of employers to the business of training volunteer soldiers.

Herefordshire's own National Reserve, the Herefordshire Company, totalled 905 men, 600 of them in the city. There were three units: the Regulars (naval and military) under Col H.R.C. Hewat (Hewat was destined to lose a son in the war); the militia under Major C.E. Wegg-Prosser (he would also lose a son); and the volunteers and territorials under Capt Bamford. That summer the Old Guard, as it was known, was called out for a church service at Tupsley by Col M.J.G. Scobie, a prominent and colourful Hereford lawyer who sometimes rode to his offices in Offa Street in full dress uniform from his home at Armdale House.

Although the parade attracted 22 sergeants and was led by the rousing music of the King Street Adult School band, only 200 soldiers turned out. Those present were invited to sign a pledge: 'I undertake in the event of imminent national danger to place my services at the disposal of His Majesty the King for home defence' (Class I) or 'foreign service as well' (Class II). One hundred and fifty men signed for 'home and foreign service', little knowing they had committed themselves to fighting in one of the worst wars in recent history.

In the light of the growing threat from Europe, the army held regular manoeuvres in the region. Sgt Jones from Weobley, Sgt-Major Lewis from Harewood End and Sgt Butcher from Ross, all members of the Army Service Corps, Mechanics Section, were pictured on manoeuvres with a traction engine and motorcycle in that August's *Hereford Times*. The local newspapers, meanwhile, were full of military news. In November Capt J.A. Hull was reported to have congratulated Leominster's non-commissioned officers and men who turned out on duty to escort the new mayor, Councillor J. Watkins, to church. 'Some men have bicycled over 12 miles to be present,' observed the captain. Towards the end of the year there were reports that a mass manoeuvre of the Expeditionary Force would be held in the region the following September with the royal family expected to join the Earl of Beauchamp at Madresfield Court to watch the action. Leominster town

Young soldiers with the 1st Herefords in training near Breinton. 'Men from this county are joining the colours every week,' reported the *Hereford Times* as tensions rose in Europe. (Photo: Pat and Don Davies)

council, sensing an opportunity for some additional income, campaigned for the former polo ground outside town to be adopted as an army camp during the manoeuvres.

As Christmas approached Lt-Col J.H. Gilbert Harris, commanding the 1st Battalion of the Herefordshire Regiment, published the names of his latest recruits ('No 1368 Boy A. Hurcomb, A. Co. and 1369 Boy C. Teague') in the local press, while Lt Col J.R. Raywood, commanding the South Wales Mounted Brigade Field Ambulance (Royal Army Medical Corps – RAMC), listed his new drivers: Sockett, Lakin, Taysom, Sgt Jordan, Ptes Roden, Adkins, Witherstone and Kennett. Not to be outdone, Hereford Cathedral School listed their latest cadet recruits: Sgt Levason and Ptes Cook, C.M. Williams, Vickers, Forward, Jones and Musgrove.

Warnings that the county, and the country, were short of army and navy volunteers were steadfastly ignored. Most people believed that the British Navy was invincible and held to the popular notion that one fighting Englishman was equal to five German soldiers. Such views were in line with those of men such as Philip Snowden, the MP for Blackburn, who believed there was no need for Britain to adopt conscription or 'universal service' as the authorities had in France and Germany. Snowden, a pacifist and an ardent supporter of women's suffrage, contended that militarism was 'a thing to be rejected'. He proposed visiting Hereford that December to share his views. It prompted the National Service League to organise a counter-meeting at Hereford Town Hall. The League enjoyed considerable support locally. Set up as a pressure group in 1902, it campaigned for compulsory universal service and military training. Its chairman, the Boer War hero Lord Roberts, had shocked the liberal press the year before with his prediction that war would take place 'the instant German forces by land and sea, are by their superiority at every point, as certain of victory as anything in human calculation'.

The Ross MP Percy Clive was among those who addressed the League supporters in Hereford, standing beneath a portrait of Lord Roberts patriotically draped with Union Jacks and, with characteristic bluntness, telling the assembled company he did not want to see the country 'overrun by Germans'. He proposed that, for the next three years, every boy of 18 should undertake four months' training with two weeks a year in camp. They would then be liable for service up to the age of 30.

His proposals were backed by another Boer War hero, Major General Sir Elliott Wood from Holmer Court and Judge Harris Lea, who warned his audience: 'I am more than ever convinced that in the interests of peace it is most necessary we should be better prepared for war than we are now.'

The men were preaching to the converted. Their audience included League supporter E.P. Bailey who had written to the *Hereford Times* earlier in November: 'If any desperate crises [*sic*] ever occurs we may be stampeded into real conscription for the Regular Army.' (It was a perceptive view: Britain would be forced to introduce conscription in 1916.) And Bailey

Major General Sir Elliott Wood. He warned of the approaching war.

attacked men like Snowden who 'blessed our late Radical Premier for halving our naval building'. He added: 'It did not suit him to finish the story that a friendly Germany promptly replied by doubling theirs.'

Bailey echoed the general feeling of disquiet, summed up by the mayor, the department store owner and estate agent George Greenland. Greenland was to play a key role on the home front in Herefordshire over the next few years. He told the Town Hall audience that, without wishing to interfere with social reform, the time had come to ensure the Territorial Force was prepared and efficient to face the situation 'as regards home and imperial defence. The nation,' he insisted, 'is not prepared for an emergency.'

So it was against a background of local militarism and national ambivalence that the county of Herefordshire headed towards what would become known as the Great War. For the rest of the year – as the management of the Garrick Theatre began to rebuild after a fire, the county's first ferro-concrete bridge was opened over the Lugg near Sutton, and 12 hunts, from the North Herefordshire down to the Llangibby, rode to the hounds – life in Herefordshire carried on much as before. Only the provincial journalist who had visited Copthorne Barracks for the *Hereford Times* offered a salutary word of comfort for what the future might hold: 'The preparations [of the King's Shropshire Light Infantry] for a sudden war are as complete as it is possible to make them.' Within a quarter of an hour the men could be equipped for battle 'down to the last button'. His prediction would be put to the test on August 4 of the following year.

Chapter 2

1914

Four years of war dawned in 1914. As hundreds of volunteers departed from county towns and villages, those left behind were soon struggling with labour shortages, spiralling prices and an economic downturn.

In the early months of 1914 the military was gearing up for action. MP William Hewins was anticipating a new year that was 'likely to be full of trouble and difficulties' when he addressed a political rally at St James' Parish Room in Hereford. He was speaking, not of a threat from Germany, but of the rising cost of living and developments in Ireland over what he called the farce of Home Rule. However, as one citizen noted in the local press, Germany alone was refusing to come to an arrangement for reducing armaments. As a consequence Weobley was hosting a military harness instruction course, Leominster a foot parade by the Welsh Division HQ and the RAMC regular meetings at Burghill Reading Room.

On Bank Holiday Monday, August 3, the *Hereford Times* replaced its customary front page of classifieds with the fateful headlines: 'England's Decision – Kaiser's Troops Enter Belgian Territory'. All naval reserves were directed to 'proceed forthwith to the ship or establishment already notified them' and a group soon gathered at Barrs Court Station, Hereford for the special train from Salop to Portsmouth, Plymouth and other

The 1st Herefordshire Rifle (reserve) Brigade drilling on Castle Green.
All signed for foreign service in September 1914. (Photo: Hereford Museum Service)

ports. 'They can't do without the Navy,' one railway porter told a reservist, noting, he told a reporter later, how grey was the naval officer's hair.

'The boys are ready to fight for good old England if necessary,' replied the old sailor.

A week later the newspaper published an honours list of 14 men from landlocked Herefordshire, ranging in rank from commander to stoker, then serving with the navy. They included Tupsley's Walter Allen, commander of *HMS Broke* and Commander Frederick Parland Loder-Symonds of *HMS Achates*; two brothers, Rowland and Hubert Chapman heading respectively for *HMS Hannibal* and *HMS Albion* (*Albion* would be involved in the Gallipoli campaign). Austin Lilley was bound for *HMS Attack*, sunk by a German U-boat in 1917, and Dick Onslow for *HMS Queen Mary*, the cruiser that would be sunk during the Battle of Jutland in 1917 with the loss of 1,266 men. Those drowned would include 28-year-old Charles Bland from Ross and 22-year-old George Lane from Withington.

Absent from the newspaper's list, however, was Joseph Gedge. The son of the former Marden vicar Revd Edmund Gedge and his wife May, Joe was staff paymaster aboard *HMS Amphion*. On 6 August his ship had struck a mine and sunk in the North Sea. *HMS Amphion* was the navy's first casualty. Joe, along with 149 other sailors, drowned. The Marden vicar's son had earned the dubious distinction of being the first officer to die in World War I.

During the early months of 1914 life had continued as before, although the news from Europe was increasingly depressing. Now, with war finally declared, there was

Brothers George and Ivor Davies and their friend Harry Hands enlisted with a group of other men from the Hereford Baptist Chapel. They are pictured here on the Castle Green in 1914. George and Harry would both be invalided out of the army later after being wounded. Harry, who was left blind, emigrated to Canada. (Photo: Pat and Don Davies)

almost a sense of relief not least because everyone was confident that Germany would be defeated within six months. 'We thought the war would be over before Christmas,' recalled Hereford tailor Percy Pritchard, who headed down to the recruitment office in Harold Street.

The customary crowds of bank holidaymakers at country railway stations had disappeared, to be replaced by groups of soldiers and sailors who crowded on to the platforms, saying their goodbyes under sunny August skies. The mass movement of troops forced the Great Western Railway to cancel all excursions. Also cancelled was the usual day off for the schoolchildren of Allensmore: their new head teacher, Adolphus Wetters, called them in and marched them down to the Tram Inn Station to see the Territorials off.

At Fawley Station meanwhile, a fresh-faced farmer's son from King's Caple was waiting for the Hereford train. Robert Bellamy was an impres-

Orcop's William Morgan had enlisted as a horse driver, working with teams of six horses in pairs. Wounded in the leg he was sent home. After the war he returned to work as a builder in Hereford, cycling to work every day from his home in Orcop. (Photo: Mary Fryer)

As an 18-year-old from Penallt, Kings Caple, Robert Bellamy left the family farm to enlist with the RAMC. (Photo: Bellamy family)

sionable 18-year-old who had recently finished his schooling at Wycliffe College. 'Some of us got together and went to the barracks in Hereford you see? We thought we should be away for a month-long spree as you might say. Instead of that we were away for four and a half years.' Robert joined the Hereford-based Field Ambulance attached to the RAMC, which, as part of the national Territorial Force, also boasted three yeomanry regiments, a horse artillery battery and an ammunition column. That August Robert and his Field Ambulance unit moved to East Anglia for training.

By his own account life at Penallt, the family's tenanted farm, had been hard, but companionable. 'It was a mixed farm, animals, sheep, pigs, the lot.' He had worked ten-hour days alongside a dozen men including a chief waggoner and his two assistants, a shepherd, cowman, general workmen and the odd-job man who lived in and looked after his father's hunters. Robert said his goodbyes and set off smartly down the shady, winding lane to Fawley Station. He was leaving a way of life that was at an end.

With labour troubles continuing to simmer in the farmyard, farmers found themselves looking at an uncertain future. Thanks to a 4% increase in that year's harvest, the Board of Agriculture and Fisheries had announced four months' stock of wheat and the news contributed to the mayor of Hereford Councillor Greenland's optimistic mood. He thought it inconceivable that the county would suffer any 'exceptional distress arising from the economic disturbance', depending, as it did, upon agriculture and not manufacturing. The Workers' Union men, however, were still bitter about the outcome of their abandoned strike. Many did not hesitate: they left the land and enlisted. Farm labourer William Powell from Pandy was among them, although, instead of enlisting when he reached Hereford, he fell in with some drinking companions, all soldiers, who told him he would be rejected because of his false teeth. The next morning a penitent and dejected Powell stood before the city magistrates and admitted to being drunk and disorderly and pinching a nurse's bicycle. (The ban on recruits with bad teeth was lifted in March 1915 and soldiers were given free dental treatment instead.)

But farm workers like Albert Fryer from Ross did not hesitate to enlist. On 16 October 1914 he signed up as a rifleman with the army. (He survived for three years and 306 days, only being discharged in the final days of the war after being gassed and shot in the arm. He went back to work for his old employer, Col Owen.) Now, as the loss of labour began to bite, Ross farmer K.M. Power of Ashton Court called for special neighbourhood committees to be set up to manage the harvests while the

An 18-year-old farm labourer from Ross, Albert Fryer (middle row standing, sixth from the right) enlisted as soon as he could with the London 18th Battalion. It was 16 October 1914. After the war he settled as a gardener in Llangarron. (Photo: Stan Fryer)

headmaster of Shrewsbury School, Revd Cyril Alington, publicly volunteered to help with the Herefordshire harvests during the school holidays. (His daughter, Lavinia, then a three-year-old, would later marry Roger Mynors of Treago Castle, St Weonards.) Like Alington, people instinctively turned to the land in a crisis. C.E. Symonds from Pengethley advised farmers to sow spare ground with turnips and cabbages and allocate 'a few extra rods of land' for their farm labourers to grow vegetables. Sherwood Smith from Clifton recommended allotment holders plant nutritious loganberry and blackberry plants while local authorities started up special neighbourhood courses on fruit bottling and produce growing. Little Marcle's Thomas Holland had his own idea on how to improve the labour problem: banning farm cider. He recommended that farmers find an extra 2 shillings a week to pay their men and abandon the traditional practice of providing them with the six to eight pints of cider most workers drank during the course of a day.

A month into the war farmers found they were losing their horses as well as their men. The District Remount office at Cagebrook in Eaton Bishop sought chargers, light draught horses and cobs, insisting that all animals put forward for purchase for the army should be 'quiet enough to handle, and run quietly in hand'. There was disappointment at Hereford Market when the remount purchaser postponed his plan to inspect 150 horses with a view to buying them for the army. In Leominster, however, Captains E.L.A. Heygate and R.L. Heygate from Docklow did brisk business buying horses for the army at the Etnam Street livery stalls. The brothers would survive the war while their near neighbours, 26-year-old Fred and 19-year-old Walter Hall, would both be killed in action.

The Heygates were closely involved with the local hunt and fox and otter hunting continued across the region, although the Ledbury Hounds' huntmaster Sir George Bullough and Mr W.S. Lane of The Farm, Bosbury had placed their hunters at the disposal of the War Office – 'and in case of need, myself', as Lane wrote to his MP.

Horse trading, in war as in peace, attracted its share of rogues. When a couple of dealers arrived at Mr S.H. Keeling's Canon Frome home claiming to be government men out to buy army mounts, Keeling became suspicious. He contacted the army and discovered that men were ordinary horse dealers hoping to turn a pound by selling the

The District Remount office at Cagebrook, Eaton Bishop advertised for chargers, light draught horses and cobs, insisting that all animals 'run quietly in hand'. (Photo: Winne Reece)

Two county blacksmiths prepare to shoe a mount. There was a high demand for war horses, and the farriers and drivers needed to service them.
LINE. (Photo: Thomas Winterbourne studio)

animals on. Meanwhile veterinary surgeon James Barking from Hereford was charged with helping himself to part of the £45 Army Horse Impressment fee due to Henry J. Pudge of Courty Park, Pixley.

By late September events in the county calendar were toppling like pub skittles. Wyeside, Tenbury, Goodrich, Pontrilas and Radnor each cancelled its annual show and, as the Bishop of Worcester declined the honour of presiding over the Three Choirs Festival (he questioned whether the consecrated house of God was a proper place for such festivities), the Festival was abandoned for the first time in almost 200 years. Some cancellations were more expedient than others. Bromyard Quoit Club, citing the war, called off its cup-tie engagement with the formidable Waunlwyd team. Hereford Quoit secretary Mr W. Magners attacked the decision describing it as 'intolerable' and accused the town of 'showing the white feather' in the face of strong opposition.

Fownhope not only shelved its annual flower show, but put plans for a motor bus service and the building of council houses and a new village hall on hold. Decisions like these were soon impacting on local businesses. Hereford builder W. Bowers (now with a score of employees at war), brickmakers Ralph Preece Davies (13 men at war, eight from Holmer Brick Works) and W.P. Lewis ('several men away') were reported to be managing as was the Hereford Steam Flour Mill and Watkins & Son's Imperial Flour Mills (their Alfred Watkins was soon to play a significant role in army recruitment). But Councillor W.G.C. Britten of Hampton Park's Hereford Brick and Tile Company warned that some of his men would have to be placed on short time because of falling

18

orders. Meanwhile cider makers W. Evans & Co (three men mobilised) and Bulmers (25 mobilised) endeavoured to manage the diminishing demand, particularly from overseas and at their busiest time of the year, by increasing hours without raising wages.

As young men like artist Brian Hatton trooped off to war (Hatton would return from the front that November to marry his fiancée Lydia Bidmead) farmers turned to the village schools as a source of potential muscle. It was still an offence for a farmer to keep a 10-year-old out of school on farm work and Sir James Rankin, chairman of the county's Education Committee, proposed that, given the current scarcity of labour, the offence should be classed as a minor misdemeanour.

There were 14,041 children on school rolls in the county, several hundred fewer than in 1913. Rankin attributed the fall to teachers removing irregular attenders from their registration books. As he explained to his committee, schools were judged on attendance records and, since poor attendance reflected badly on a school, teachers were inclined to massage the figures. Rankin was wrong: country boys were often happier turning hay bales than the pages of a school textbook and their hard-pressed families were grateful for any extra money a child could earn. Absenteeism continued to rise throughout the war.

Older boys were also persuaded to leave the classroom, albeit temporarily, by the new business of Scouting. The national Scout leader, Robert Baden-Powell, had written to local employers and the Education Committee asking them to excuse attendance for Boy Scouts so that the boys could, under the direction of the chief constable, carry messages, guard bridges and telegraph lines and watch out for spies. One city scoutmaster asked bike owners to hand their machines in at Hereford YMCA so that his lads could better patrol the roads and railway lines. (The vicar of Holmer publicly thanked parishioners who gave board to Scouts guarding the Leominster road during August.)

Meanwhile, suspicions were easily aroused. That autumn there were rumours of a German having being arrested in Ledbury. Believed to be in the motor trade, he was said to have been seen sketching local roads and landmarks. In Hereford, City Councillor E.J. Peters called for local Germans to be treated in a considerate manner, but a German from Cardiff who called in at Leominster's Royal Oak found himself summarily frogmarched to the police station by the Royal Oak's customers. The duty policeman explained that the gentleman had already reported himself: the crowd demanded that he be searched. He duly consented and nothing was found.

There was similar trouble at Allensmore. Having marched his charges to the station to watch the Territorials depart, the head teacher Adolphus Wetters now found himself accused of having German ancestry. Wetters, who had been drafted in to replace a striking teacher in 1914, was not a popular man. Despite his strenuous denials, rumours of his dubious past continued to circulate until a group of angry mothers descended on the school. Wetters rashly let them in through the school gates and the resulting confrontation between himself and the parents turned into a minor riot, which was only brought under control by the arrival of the police. Wetters was hastily moved to Bromyard school by the Education Committee.

Young men who were too old for school and too young to enlist were both excited and frustrated. 'We thought that we'd never get abroad and we nearly mutinied,' remembered Percy Pritchard. Arthur Reed would not wait. With his older brother William already in the army, Arthur slipped out of the house and signed up with the Monmouthshire Regiment. The recruitment officer turned a blind eye to Arthur's obvious youth: the boy was 14. Arthur later visited a photographer's studio and posed in an ill-fitting uniform and a too-large cap with two friends or brothers. The boy soldier, who would later settle with his family in Stonebow Road, Hereford, served in and survived two World Wars. William Reed died at Gallipoli in 1916.

Newspaper readers settled in their armchairs to assess the odds as outlined by the *Hereford Times*: the Triple Entente (Great Britain with 720,000 men, France with 4,500,000 and Russia with 5,400,000) was facing up to 'that menace to civilisation' Germany (4,350,000 men) and 'that catspaw of Germany', Austria (3,500,000). Italy, for the time being, was neutral. It was a position that would have been untenable in Britain. 'To have remained neutral would have made us the scorn of the world,' declared a *Hereford Times* leader writer. The Bishop of Hereford disagreed. Dr John Percival, a man who championed the cause of adult education (he had chaired the first meeting of the Workers Educational Association 11 years earlier),

Arthur Reed was born in 1900 and signed up to fight with the Kings Shropshire Light Infantry in 1914. The boy soldier survived the war, married wife Lillian and worked as an engineer at Rotherwas. He died in 1970 leaving behind a son and four daughters including Jeanette Bates: 'He was a lovely quiet man who never talked about the war.' (Photo: Jeanette Bates)

was looking forward to celebrating his 80th birthday in September, but celebrations were soured when he unwisely told the *Daily News and Leader* on the eve of war: 'I feel that our Government is in duty bound to keep England strictly neutral.'

His was a lone voice of local dissent and it may have been no coincidence that the army chose to commandeer his horse shortly after he made his views known. The bishop received short shrift from his colleague on the Close, the Revd Canon Hastings Rashdall, dean of Hereford. The dean spoke out against the bishop during a service of intercession in the cathedral that August. A military parade, led by the RAMC, had marched through High Town to the cathedral, accompanied by the City Military Band, 60 women from the British Red Cross, Boy Scouts and youngsters from the Working Boys Home. Once inside, the 3,500-strong congregation listened to the dean thunder: 'It is too late to talk of neutrality.'

Men such as Sidney Smith, the local pig killer at St Owens Cross, responded to the call to arms. (Photo: Mary Fryer)

Internee Percy Hull

Dr Percival was forced to retract. In an off-the-record interview with the local press he explained that he had been 'misled by Ministers' and now gave his backing to the war, 'terrible as it is likely to be'. His own son, Lt A.J.B. Percival would soon be serving in France.

Absent from the controversy in the cathedral that day was the organist and friend of Edward Elgar, Percy C. Hull. Earlier in July Hull had arranged a fund-raising concert at Hereford Training College before departing for what turned out to be an unwise choice for a holiday destination: Germany. North Herefordshire's former MP, Edmund Lamb, had also been caught holidaying behind enemy lines, but managed to catch the last train out of Austria. News of these continental difficulties was regularly communicated by telegram to the Constitutional Club in East Street and posted on their notice board: the club became a busy meeting place.

Percy Hull was less fortunate than Edmund Lamb. Although his sister received a postcard assuring her of his imminent return, he was arrested by the Germans and taken to Ruhleben Internment Camp where he was interned along with three thousand others. Because they were internees rather than prisoners of war, the inmates ran the camp, a former racecourse, themselves, living in isolation and organising garden clubs and theatrical and musical events to entertain one another. Many were left with feelings of profound guilt when, three years later, they were released and allowed home.

At home, recruitment continued along with many military-style memorial services. At Ledbury reservists were joined by the First Putley Boy Scouts, the Lad's Church Brigade and the town band as they marched through town to St Michael's Church. But, as Lord Roberts had predicted, it was too little, too late and with the British Expeditionary Force fighting a rearguard action in Belgium, Lord Kitchener called for a second army of 100,000 men. His letter, received at the Hereford recruiting office, identified one key group: unmarried men under the age of 42. Recruitment began in earnest.

Three senior officers took charge of recruitment in Herefordshire: the colourful Col Scobie, the dean of Hereford's son-in-law Sir Richard Butler, and the squire of Lugwardine Court, 46-year-old Sir Herbert Archer Croft. Their methods were comprehensive and thorough. Having consulted with the Lord Lieutenant Sir John Cotterell at Garnons, Scobie called for representatives from all the rural districts to a meeting at the Kemble Theatre in Broad Street one Sunday evening in late August. A committee was formed which would oversee 17 districts, each divided into its respective parishes: Hereford City and rural, Bromyard, Dore, Kington urban and rural, Eardisley, Ledbury urban and rural, Leintwardine, Leominster borough and rural, Ross urban and rural, Weobley, Staunton on Wye and Whitchurch.

Recruitment meetings were convened in every meeting room and parish hall in Herefordshire. Each involved Scobie, Butler, Croft or Cotterell joining any local gentry on temporary stages hung with Union Jacks and lined with straight-backed chairs. Recruiting officers in uniform stood to one side as guest speakers gave stirring and patriotic speeches. Sometimes encouraging letters from serving soldiers would be read out: 'We are eagerly awaiting the order to go to the Front,' wrote Capt R. Greatrex-Yates in one such letter addressed to Ross Town Council. Would-be volunteers were then asked to step forward and sign up with the recruiting officer or be taken direct to the nearest recruiting office. Afterwards, as refreshments were laid on, the audience would be entertained by amateur performers, accompanied on the piano, singing patriotic songs. Some country lads took the King's shilling if only to enjoy a car ride: several car owners took up Cotterell's suggestion that they ferry young enlisters to the recruiting offices in their cars. (There were red faces at Harewood End police station when a dutiful, but suspicious constable stopped and searched a car late one night near Whitchurch. It contained Scobie and Butler, returning from one such recruitment meeting.)

Scobie, Croft and Butler managed to secure a Daimler van, its sides plastered with recruitment posters, which was sent on a tour of the countryside reminding villagers of the need to go and 'fight the Hun'. The names of volunteers were passed on to newspaper editors who published them as rolls of honour.

Within a month Hereford and its satellite towns of Ledbury, Leominster, Ross, Bromyard and Kington were altered beyond belief, according to an observer on the *Hereford Times*, which with rising paper prices had been reduced from 16 to 12 pages. 'As the children return from school, all excite[ed] about the war, yonder is a military officer in khaki mounted on a horse only a day or two ago commandeered from a gentleman's private residence … a squad of local recruits marching to the Drill Hall or the Barracks for enlistment and a section of [the] Ambulance Corps rigged out with vehicles that one seems to recognise despite their coats of war paint.'

The paintwork was usually applied by Messrs C. & J. Jones, motor body builders from Edgar Street, which had itself been commandeered for seven days to equip the vehicles

Troops passing along a rainy Ledbury High Street. 1914 proved to be the wettest year on record.
(Photo: Herefordshire Museum Service)

requisitioned from tradespeople and converted to carry stretchers. The company assured newspaper readers that once this vital work was complete they would again be at the disposal of their regular customers.

Mrs A.W. Foster from Brockhampton Court chose to send to the front not only her Daimler car, registration CJ 245 and converted for ambulance work by Messrs Jones, but also her head chauffeur. 'The car is doing excellent work accompanied by Mr Hedges, Mrs Foster's head chauffeur ... conveying wounded to Paris,' reported one local newspaper. The following year George Butcher of Belmont Road, Hereford, a former chauffeur to Mrs Foster, received a letter from his friend, a Garway man, Arthur Webb of the Fifth Siege Battery, to say he had seen Mrs Foster's Daimler 'passing through a small town I know several times. This,' he added, 'is a fine life and I would advise any chauffeur who likes adventure to give it a go.' Arthur, who had himself been a chauffeur at James Fryer's garage in Hereford, added: 'I am still in the land of the living: it has been a long and trying winter.' (Mr and Mrs Foster's second son, 23-year-old Lt Cedric Foster would be killed in France the following spring.)

Recruitment continued in the build-up to what became one of the wettest winters on record. Over 500 men and 21 officers enlisted although, curiously, 150 Territorials were later sent back to the city from the 1st Battalion Herefordshire Regiment without their equipment or badges. According to press reports many of them had been judged temporarily medically unfit (there had been an outbreak of measles). In late September Captain Hill, in charge of the Welsh Division of the Army Service Corps (ASC) asked for 72 drivers. Scobie promptly recruited 60 including Lt Harold James, the son of

Hereford's Alderman James. Meanwhile educated volunteers were invited to enlist in one of the proposed new five battalions of public school and university men. They were directed to contact Mr E.F. Bulmer at the ciderman's offices in Ryeland Street.

Towards the end of the year 60 members of the RAMC were instructed to assemble in front of the Green Dragon in Broad Street, Hereford before their commanding officer, Lt-Col J.R.I. Raywood. Seven months earlier, in peacetime, the RAMC's Herefordshire contingent, enjoying its annual dinner at the Imperial Café in the city, was reported to have 64 men, a few stretchers, haversacks 'and mighty little else except what the men brought themselves', according to Raywood. The unit was now up to strength and fully equipped as Raywood called to his men lined up on Broad Street: 'How many of you will volunteer for Imperial Service?' To a man they all stepped forward as, a local reporter noted, 'all thought of the loved ones they might be called upon to leave behind sank into insignificance'.

The sister of one volunteer was approached by the reporter. How did she feel? he asked. 'I'm sorry he has volunteered to go abroad, but if he had not done so, I should have given him a piece of my mind! I don't want it to be said that a brother of mine is a coward.' The Hereford girl summed up the general feeling. As the popular women's recruiting song, *Your King and Country Want You*, went: 'Oh we don't want to lose you, but we think you ought to go.'

The pressure to enlist intensified. In Whitecross, Hereford, 100 parishioners had already volunteered to fight when the vicar, Revd Douglas Sargent, published a fresh appeal in the parish newsletter: 'Parents! Do not keep your sons back. Sweethearts! Do not keep your young men back,' he wrote. 'It is a glorious thing to fight, yea, and if need be, to lay down one's life for one's country.'

The names of volunteers were pinned up in public often on parish church doors. St James' Church in Hereford proudly posted a list of 29 men who had left to serve King and Country. They included the vicar's two sons, F.R. Landsell of the Royal Naval Reserve and J.A.D. Landsell of the Artists' Rifles Corps. There were several navy men including Joseph Manning, Harry Hooper (*HMS Monarch*), Vincent C. Bullen (*HMS Vanguard*) and A. Boswell (*HMS Implacable*). *Monarch* and *Vanguard* turned out to be 'lucky ships', naval vessels that pulled through the war without serious damage. An accident involving munitions aboard *HMS Vanguard*, however, saw the ship explode at Scapa Flow in 1917 killing chief stoker Vincent Bullen and 834 of his fellow sailors. It was one of the worst accidents ever suffered by the Royal Navy.

Patriotic parents with several sons on the front line became news items. Mrs E. Bodman of 132 St Owen Street described how all four of her sons and two nephews, whom she had looked after since they were small, were serving with the colours. The Burghill landlord of the Tow Tree Inn, Fred Wilkins, told how his three sons had all enlisted and recently found themselves sharing a railway carriage in another part of the country with two Hereford boys, the sons of Alderman E.L. Wallis, Trooper George from the Berkshire Yeomanry and Lt Owen with the Herefordshire Territorials. (Two of Fred Wilkins' sons, Fred and Percy, were destined to die on the Western Front.)

The rail companies had been brought under government control that August. They were now pressed into service to bring refugees from Belgium into the county. Capt

Clive had already written to Mayor Greenland warning him to expect 50 Belgian civilians 'of the better class of refugees, for at least a week'. Several Herefordians generously offered accommodation including Brian Hatton's family at Mount Craig, a Mr Jay at Mordiford post office and two cider makers, H.P. Bulmer at Longmeadow and Mr R.E. Ridler at Clehonger. In the event only two families, one the Stoofs of Louvain, arrived at Barrs Court Station aboard the 7.27pm from Paddington. They were outnumbered by their reception committee: Mayor Greenland, Mrs Hewat of The Elms, Aylestone Hill, Mrs E.C. Guerney and the Misses Newton from Hampton Park. Soon, however, more displaced Belgian families arrived including a group of 13, described by the *Hereford Journal* as 'of a superior type'. They were taken to Kilforge, the Ballingham home of Chief Constable Frank Richardson. A refugee wrote later: 'We consider Hereford a paradise.'

At least one newspaper correspondent wondered if the refugees might undertake some unpaid work in return for their keep. It prompted a swift retort from the Workers' Union's Sidney Box who insisted the Belgians should be paid 'at the standard rate'. This served to upset another correspondent to the newspapers who demanded that English jobs be reserved for English people. It was left to the War Refugee Committee to offer guidance and recommend that the guests be given only gifts, charity and odd jobs. That autumn at least one Belgian refugee, Professor Stoofs, was making himself useful by offering French and Flemish speaking lessons along with a Mrs D. West, who was of French descent, to Herefordshire soldiers heading for France.

Another 30 refugees arrived in October including one poor widow who, according to a newspaper report, had not only lost her husband, but witnessed a German shoot her mother-in-law ('the barbarians practically blew her head off'). In Ledbury the Territorial Hall was set aside for Belgian refugees and when 50 wounded Belgian soldiers, dressed in their best blue uniforms, arrived from Cardiff at Barrs Court Station they were driven to the hospital through streets lined with cheering crowds.

(The encounters sometimes led to romance. Reg Robins from the Herefordshire Regiment was fighting the Germans in a small Belgian town during the Second World War when a voice called out: 'How's Hereford doing?' An elderly lady was standing on her doorstep, her arms crossed, ignoring the crossfire. 'She'd seen my badge,' Reg remembered. 'Turned out she'd been at school with my mum in St Owens, Hereford and gone as a nurse during the first war. She had fallen in love with this wounded Belgian soldier and after the war come over and married him. I wanted to find out her name, but we were moved on. I never saw her again.')

The chauffeurs ferrying the wounded to hospital were volunteers, members of Herefordshire Automobile Club. In 1913 they had assembled outside the Mitre Hotel in Broad Street before heading off on noisy rallies and leisure drives through the countryside. Now more than 50 drivers were helping businesses where vehicles had been requisitioned, or ferrying volunteers who wanted to enlist to the barracks under the organising hand of their club secretary, by coincidence a Mr Carless of Bridge Street, Hereford.

The Mitre Hotel was also the suggested venue for a shooting club. Its proprietor, Mr T. Downing, proposed it as a meeting place for older men prepared to take rifle-shooting

Until the outbreak of war, Hereford's motoring enthusiasts regularly met in Broad Street before heading off into the country. Members of the Automobile Club were soon volunteering themselves and their cars for war work. (Photo: Derrick Blake)

lessons. They could, he explained, assist in the protection of the county in the event of a German invasion. Major General Sir Elliott Wood poured scorn on the plan. In the event of a German invasion, he wrote to one newspaper, such men would be 'shot like dogs and bring down savage reprisals on their villages'. Mr Downing's plan was not taken up.

A more successful notion was the creation of a motorcycle club and their members placed themselves, together with their bikes, at the disposal of the police. Police ranks had been substantially increased by the recruitment of a small army of special constables. Two months into the war, 157 men had volunteered at Hereford police station including Councillors E.R. Dymond, E.W. Langford and H.R. Rogers. They were dispatched to administer the new responsibilities required by war. Under the Official Secrets Act, for example, landlords were forbidden to serve soldiers after 9pm. The provisions did not apply to civilians like Rose Jones who, having had one too many that autumn, was arrested by the police. Hauled up before the magistrates charged with being drunk and disorderly she was let off with a caution after she explained to the bench: 'My brother went away to the war.'

Police were often called to deal with problems arising out of the soldiers billeted in a camp near Hereford. Apart from the occasional case of orchard robbing, the police had to be called to break up a fight when food-stall owner Robert Wall was accused of selling German sausages to Territorials strolling by. Wall, who denied the accusation, had been assaulted by an outraged member of the public, James Morgan. The camp was out of bounds to civilians, but the khaki proved a magnet to some girls including

Louisa Hall from Kimbolton, Bella Miler from Gaol Street, Hereford and three girls from Smethwick who were sent home from the camp after being brought before the magistrates. The court was told they were 'of a class of women who were following the camp, and were an intolerable nuisance'.

A group of travelling European musicians caught up in Hereford by the war proved less a nuisance and more of an inconvenience. The Hungarian Band had been regular visitors to Britain – they had been entertaining the public with concerts on Hereford's Castle Green for over 20 years – and they were performing in the city that autumn when war broke out. They were now marooned, without their instruments, which had been sent on ahead. Some bandsmen began busking on begged or borrowed instruments, but their music failed to soften the heart of John Bull, as he signed himself in the letters column of the *Hereford Times*: 'Why are foreigners of this class allowed to play in our streets for the purpose of begging while an Englishman asking for a crust of bread is locked up?'

This appeared to be a reference to the journeymen or roadsters who, as another letter writer put it, 'nightly slink into Hereford Workhouse'. (The author signed himself 'Patriot'.) There had been fewer journeymen on the roads since the start of war, although Abbey Dore Guardians Mr A.S. Wood and Revd P. Cave-Moyle still found their existence distressing. The vicar, who was shortly to leave for the front to serve as an army chaplain, counted six on his way to one Guardians' meeting and thought it 'a crying shame' to see these fellows about when the army was short of men.

That October the Hereford Guardians agreed the half-yearly 'requisite of £11,700 for the Workhouse' (it was down from £14,300 the previous year), Mr W.G. Bankes attacking government orders for the improved treatment of tramps as 'only giving more to the thriftless at the expense of the thrifty'. He told his fellow committee members: 'The large majority of these fellows who loaf along the roads calling at houses don't want food; they want money and when they get it they spend it in the public houses.' 'Patriot' proposed a chilling solution, one that would be adopted by the German Third Reich in 25 years' time: 'Casuals', he said, should be used as forced labour on the harvest, any resistance being met with corporal punishment or having the unfortunates placed in a compound 'where the old Biblical rule should apply: "if a man will not work neither shall he eat"'.

Matters, meanwhile, had worsened for the Hungarian music makers. For a while they were required to register as aliens and report regularly to Hereford police station. In October they were formally arrested and sent to a concentration camp in Cardiff. Sailors Rudolph Novack and Antonio Krukov suffered a similar fate when they were stopped near Ledbury. The victims of new wartime shipping rules, Novack and Krukov had lost their jobs as crewmen aboard a British steamship after an order was implemented allowing only British subjects to be employed. Destitute and unable to return home, the sailors had travelled up to Herefordshire looking for farm work on hop and fruit picking when they were arrested. They were dispatched to Cardiff, but not before one of the magistrates, Mr Watkins, made a donation of 2s 6d towards their expenses. There was also some sympathy from the bench when a 34-year-old collier and former Austrian army soldier, Oscar Schilham, was brought before them. He had strayed beyond the permitted five miles from his registered home as a hop picker at Bishops Frome.

The pressure to enlist was intensifying. Several local women had taken up the white feather campaign, started by a group of Folkestone women and designed to humiliate men not in uniform. As Robert Bellamy recalled: 'If you went to Ross [market] for instance, and you'd got nothing to show that you were in the services, you were given a white feather.' There was worse to come. 'Aunt Fanny', as she styled herself in letters to the local press, proposed publishing her 'petticoat list' of shirkers. When, by the end of September, newspapers carried the full list of over 1,000 Herefordshire men now 'with the Fleet or with the colours', Aunt Fanny wrote demanding the names of 'shirkers' for her Petticoat List, promising alarmingly, 'we women know who's who'. It prompted one 28-year-old from 163 Belmont Road to point out that he was caring for his mother and his father who was crippled while his brother was serving with the RAMC. 'Would your sneering Petticoats and white feather young ladies say it is my duty to enlist or to remain at home? I think if the Government made it worthwhile they would soon get plenty of men.'

The war provided women who could afford to do so the chance to volunteer for useful work. That autumn the national suffragette leader Millicent Fawcett had announced the suspension of ordinary political work in the face of the national crisis and called on members to devote their efforts to help those suffering from the war. A 'Herefordshire woman', as she signed herself in the *Hereford Times*, exhorted her sisters to bear with fortitude the rise in grocery prices and concentrate on producing nourishing and cheap stews, soups and puddings. She also urged them to volunteer for the Red Cross (public donations to the Hereford branch had recently raised £525), while Lilian Capper volunteered to collect any surplus dairy and game for the Red Cross at her home, The Northgate in St Weonards. A nurse Lewis from Pool Farm, Hereford, meanwhile, offered advice to women stitching underclothes for wounded soldiers – 'any roughness in seam or stitches is apt to irritate'.

Sir Archer Croft stepped down from his recruitment duties and as chairman of the Hospital Committee in order to rejoin his regiment, but not before calling on ladies, especially those with a hospital certificate, to offer their services to Hereford's General Hospital. The hospital, which had already seen several nurses and the house surgeon Dr Lloyd depart for active service, was dealing with around 120 patients a month. That autumn they set aside 60 beds for wounded soldiers, the general board of management agreeing to charge the War Office 3 shillings a day for the treatment of wounded men. There was to be no charge for soldiers from the Herefordshire Territorials. Meanwhile, women who signed up to provide field nursing with the Voluntary Aid Detachment (VAD) were being dispatched for training to the county's VAD hospitals: Hampton Grange and Beechwood Red Cross Hospital in Hereford; Hightree House in Leintwardine; Sarnesfield Court Red Cross Hospital, Sarnesfield near Weobley; The Upper Hall, Ledbury; Hampton Court Hospital, Leominster; Caradoc Court at Sellack; and Red Cross hospitals at Kington, Colwall and Bromyard. Set up by the Joint War Committee, a joint organisation run by the Red Cross and the Order of St John of Jerusalem, and funded on a daily allowance from the War Office, they were often run by the house owners themselves: the 27-bed Hightree House was managed by its owner Miss Gertrude Crawshay with her neighbour, Mrs Jebb. Others in the neighbourhood volunteered to help paid staff such as the cooks in caring for the patients. The soldiers, generally less seriously injured than their comrades in the military hospitals, preferred the relaxed and homely atmosphere of the VAD hospital.

Local photographers found themselves enjoying a surge of new business as women took on their new roles and men donned khaki. In Gloucester Road, Ross, Colman Debenham competed for the trade with Mr R.E. Davies, Mr Davies gaining some advantage from a rumour that Debenham was a German. Debenham was obliged to write to the *Ross Gazette* begging to be allowed to 'contradict the statement that I am German or come from German descent'. Back in Hereford photographer W.H. Bustin was erecting his tripod outside the west door of the cathedral to capture the colours of the 1st Battalion Herefordshire Regiment being carried inside for safe keeping. He listed the duty guard in his notebook including the names of Sir Archer Croft and Pte Geoffrey Bulmer (neither of whom would survive the war). As the colours were carried out of the sunlight into the dim interior of the cathedral it was as if the family silver was being stowed away in anticipation of some dreadful event.

No one doubted that war would cause significant casualties and as Ross citizens raised almost £100 for the Soldiers' and Sailors' Families Association, funds began flooding in for a National Relief Fund. Set up by the Prince of Wales the fund was designed to meet any distress caused by the war and to assist the wives and families of territorials and soldiers and sailors (but not, initially at least, their common-law wives). The Relief Committee was to be represented by a weighty 52 volunteers who were invited to join the Relief Committee led by Mayor Greenland. Its member-ship of churchmen, councillors, MPs, trade unionists and newspaper editors reflected the upper echelons of local society and they were quick to set a tone of being firm but fair. Councillor H.P. Bulmer, for one, warned against giving charity in cash. It was impor-tant, he stressed, to know the condi-tion of the people assisted.

The recruitment of men and women gave a business boost to local photographers, including the studio of W.H. Bustin. (Photo: Herefordshire Libraries)

Mayor Greenland, still blithely optimistic, remained convinced that there was 'no immediate distress in Herefordshire, nor likely to be for some time' although he agreed to assist in the organising of district committees to cover the whole county. Almost immediately Ledbury's all-male committee came in for criticism after refusing the generous offer of 2,500lbs of jam, made by the Ledbury Domestic Science school, to be sold for the cost of the sugar alone to the working people of Ledbury. Mr C.C. Radcliffe-Cooke of Much Marcle took a dim view of this 'act of singular ineptitude', castigating the committee men as 'an insult to the intelligence of the women of Ledbury'.

The local relief fund rapidly topped £2,000, its donors spurred on by the press publishing congratulatory lists of benefactors together with the amount of each donation. Heading the list was a gift of £500 from Sir Robert and Lady Lucas-Tooth, who threw open Holme Lacy Park for a fundraising party (a notice was posted in the local press advising guests of convenient train times in order for them to attend). The Lucas-Tooths were spurred on by having two of their three sons, the 33-year-old Capt Douglas and 35-year-old Capt Selwyn already serving in France, Douglas in the cavalry with the Queen's Royal Lancers and Selwyn with the Lancashire Fusiliers. That September Douglas was killed in action. A month later Selwyn was killed. Sir Robert never recovered from the shock. He died the following February.

The fund was not the only draw on people's purses. Louise Luard of South Bank House launched her own appeal for tobacco, chocolate, pencils, writing paper and acid drops ('in tins') for the KSLI. Her husband, Major Luard, had reported that the nights were very cold and that gifts of mittens, mufflers and warm gloves were much appreciated. Eleanor Hereford was collecting flannel shirts and socks on behalf of her brother, Sir Robert Cockburn of the 7th Battalion, KSLI; Mrs Ely of Pyon House collected for the 1st Battalion Worcester Regiment, which had returned home after two years' service in Egypt and were in urgent need of warm clothing; Mrs George Rolleston, meanwhile, was collecting for the Indian troops. Ella Mary Leather from Castle House, Weobley, whose *Folk-Lore of Herefordshire* had been published three years earlier, appealed for winter comforts to be sent to her solicitor husband Lt-Col Francis H. Leather of the Welsh Divisional Transport and Supply Company. (Their son John, who was about to enlist, had just turned 20. He would not survive the war.)

With her husband Herbert in training on the east coast with the 1st Battalion Herefordshire Regiment (he had enlisted as a lowly private) and her daughters helping with the Red Cross, Lady Croft launched her own appeal from the family seat at Lugwardine Court: a Christmas Dinner fund for men from the Herefordshire Regiment who, by December, were digging defensive trenches in case of invasion on the windswept east coast.

Fundraising was not confined to the well-heeled. Indian troops were sent £2 10 shillings collected by local hop pickers, while the villagers of Bodenham cancelled the annual harvest tea and instead donated £9 to the war effort. Some eyebrows were raised below stairs when 'servant women' were invited to contribute to Miss Bamford's shilling fund – Herefordshire's servants were quite as patriotic as their employers. Miss Bamford of Lawnswood, Hampton Park intended her funds for soldiers' socks and her efforts were duly noted in the press when the shilling fund topped £13. The donors, some of whom earned little more than 10 shillings a week, remained anonymous, listed only as '6 maids at Southbank' or '3 maids at Canon Palmer's'.

Domestics' eyebrows were raised further by employers who, with the forethought and finances to stock up on essentials such as sugar and coal, started doing so. Prices were rising. The London Coal Exchange, which reported having 'reasonable stocks at present', had predicted a price hike should war be declared. There was also bad news on the Greenock Exchange, which handled sugar imports, when the cancellation of continental shipments of sugar beet saw the price of sugar soar by £3 per ton.

A regular letter writer to the newspapers, Sherwood Smith, condemned such price increases as 'an act of cruelty and selfishness' while members of Hereford's Master Bakers' Association resolutely refused to supply more than the 'ordinary demands' of customers, an action which they claimed had pegged the rise in the price of a quarter loaf of bread (6½d) to one halfpenny. Other retailers sought to reassure their public. 'Don't Be Alarmed! No lack of meat at Cresswell and Sons' ran one advertisement as more householders turned to substituting such items as kidney beans for meat. The Hereford tailors, King and Sons, also pledged 'No advance in prices' and offered special patriotic rates on the cloth required for making up nurses' uniforms. Only the price of beer, it seemed, was immune to the vagaries of war with Gurney's bottled Whitebread Ales at 2 shillings and 6d a pint and Tennet's Lager 3 shillings and 9d.

It was little comfort to the average working woman who was finding it increasingly hard to balance the household budget. One letter to the newspapers appealed for advice on how to help a mother struggling to manage after both her sons enlisted. Another letter writer complained about the inadequate 'separation allowance' paid to corporation employees. 'There are a great many like myself,' he wrote, 'who would enlist any day if we could get enough money for our needs without applying for relief.' He pointed out that his wife and three children would receive only 18 shillings and 3d a week if he enlisted.

There was also the issue of whether or not employers would hold open the jobs of enlisted employees and provide support for their relatives for the duration of the war. Gurney's with two men away (including Alderman Gurney's own son) had benefited from army contracts and pledged to keep the jobs open and wages paid 'in the interval'. This prompted the Co-op (two men away) to do the same, unlike the India and China Tea Co. which employed 80 workers and had six shop men in the army. They reported only that they were 'considering' the question. Local seamstresses and dressmakers were said to be particularly hard hit by the economic downturn, according to the newly formed County War Distress Committee under its chairman Col Prescott Decie who also chaired the county council. Other working women had to contend with employers imposing extended periods of unpaid holiday to reduce their costs. A radical solution, proposed by Dorothy Dymond of Hampton Grange and Katherine Harley in a joint letter to the *Hereford Times*, was for women to take the place of men in offices, shops and factories. Dymond, whose husband would become mayor of Hereford, was known to be sympathetic to the aspirations of working women.

By September the first significant battles of the war had taken place and several members of the hospital board, concerned that the hospital would shortly be overwhelmed by the numbers of wounded soldiers returning to the city, offered their own homes for convalescent purposes, Col and Mrs Hewat amongst them. The Hewats had yet to learn of the death of their son, 29-year-old Anthony Hewat (he had recently married the vicar of Letton's daughter), who was killed in action at the start of September.

Yet the war still seemed far away. In late autumn one rail traveller confessed to being astonished to find himself face to face with 200 German prisoners of war, bound for internment in Scotland, while he waited on the platform at Barrs Court Station. He told a local reporter that the men looked 'quite happy and contented' and had developed a 'thirst that will not be quenched by anything except honest British beer', which they were calling for loudly from their carriages. Later he encountered a second party of Germans, ships' crews who had been seized from a fleet of German merchant vessels in Newport and who 'looked out of the carriage window in a wistful silence. This', suggested the reporter, 'is bringing the war close to our doors.'

In spite of the speeches, the recruitment drives and the sea of khaki, there was little sense of what this war was really like. Fed only by rumours (one held that the Germans were so short of uniforms that their dead were buried naked but for their shirts; another whisper claimed British troops in the trenches subsisted on a daily diet of a single herring and a ration of jam) the newspapers launched an appeal for letters from the front. The initial accounts were unusually graphic: 'A shell exploded near us followed by a terrible cry,' wrote a French soldier quoted in the *Hereford Times*. 'One man had both his legs blown off, and was still alive and conscious, imploring us to kill him. An officer ran past and after a short look at the man, shot him through the heart. At that moment [the officer] got a bullet in the mouth.'

Bombardier H.S. Yapp wrote home to 78 Cotterell Street: 'The Germans were so strong and they are devils. They killed our wounded and fired our hospitals, but [the war] will soon be over as it cannot last out.' He offered the calculation that wars invariably came to an end once casualties reached 20% of the fighting strength: given that the Germans had reportedly lost 200,000 men in the first three weeks of war, conjectured one correspondent in late September, the war would be over by early October.

Former printer L/Cpl Dick Davies with the Duke of Cornwall's Light Infantry wrote to his parents in Hom Green of the day he was caught by an attack in a vineyard. He had, he said, strict instructions not to touch the grapes. 'I had the good fortune to hear about a dozen screamers [shells] coming at once and something seemed to tell me to get down. In all probability [it] saved my life. A shell burst about seven yards on the other side of me. We lost about 35 killed that day.'

Pte E. Fleetwood, another Hom Green man, was with the First Scots Guards, part of the British Expeditionary Force. During the Battle of Aisne he was wounded in the thigh by a bullet. 'I lay by the roadside for some seven hours before being found. I little thought I should come from there alive.' He added thoughtfully: 'There will certainly have to be a day of reckoning when the war is over.'

There was the occasional piece of positive news. Lt Sidney Phelps wrote to his father F.W. Phelps of Eign Street about how the armoured cruiser on which he served, *HMS Carnarvon*, had captured the German liner *Professor Warrman* with its £250,000 cargo in August. 'Our ship's company will get £200,000 prize money. It will work out at about £5 for me, but it will be a long time before we shall get it.'

Pte A. Warrell of the King's Royal Rifle Company wrote to his father, Mr S.H. Warrell, in what was described as a 'breezy letter from a Mordiford solider'. 'Our trenches were on the edge of a wood. The Germans shelled them. Talk of a warm corner. It makes you think of home a bit now and again. Nobody allowed above ground now. A company of ours was billeted in the top of a house till an eight-inch shell came through the roof and burst. It shifted 78 of our lads, 15 of them killed.'

Otto Bromfield from the Royal Engineers Signal Service wrote to his brother at 88 Park Street, Hereford that he was 'not worrying, but taking things as they come. I've slept in barns, woods, stores, cinemas, casinos, dock sheds and under the stars. We are outnumbered sometimes 10,000 to 2,000 but our boys stick to them. The Maxims [machine guns] have cut them down like corn, and when we charge with fixed bayonets see 'em run like rats. Their dead were so thick that their reinforcements couldn't advance over the top. Of course,' he added as a sombre afterthought, 'we lost too.' Published in early September, Otto's letter accurately reflected the situation during the Battle of Mons that August, the first major clash between British and German forces. The names of those killed, injured or missing, however, had yet to reach home and in the absence of more concrete news the *Hereford Times* started to speculate in October, reminding readers of officers with local connections ('Maj Cawley, Maj V.R. Brooke') who were serving in these danger zones.

Initial reports of missing men, Second Lt R.H.M. Lee and Capt C.V. Beresford, were published on 12 September. (Beresford would survive the war, having been wounded and taken prisoner.) But, one by one, reports of those killed started to appear in the newspaper columns. When the death of Major John Cawley, the third son of Sir Fred Cawley of Berrington Hall, was announced, the *Hereford Times* devoted 14 lines to his death. The newspaper also noted the death of naval paymaster Joe Gedge drowned at the start of the war. (Joe's brother Peter would be killed the following year in October, his name being added to the Cathedral Boys' memorial in the cathedral. A third brother, Basil, an army chaplain, died three years after Joe in August 1917.) Although he too died in the early days of fighting, the death of 42-year-old Major C.A.L. Yate of Madeley, Shropshire, the brother of Miss Yate of Brightwell House, Whitehorse Street, was not reported until early October, in the same issue as the death was announced of Col and Mrs Hewat's son, Capt Hewat. (Yate would be awarded the Victoria Cross: he had cut his own throat and died to avoid capture by the Germans.)

On 26 October the *Hereford Times* devoted a third of a page to the deaths of three men: Capt Douglas Lucas-Tooth, Capt Gerald Lea, son of Judge Harris Lea, and Pte A.S. Wright. Hundreds turned out for Wright's funeral and the cortege for the ex-Eign Brook Advent schoolboy and former Mansion House employee wound its way down Widemarsh Street.

Lady Croft wrote a letter of condolence to Lea's wife from Lugwardine Court: 'My dear Brenda, I hope you will forgive me for troubling you with a letter but I should like to tell you how deeply we all feel for you.' Before his death Gerald Lea had written a stream of letters to his wife Brenda, a shy beauty and daughter of the founder of the Wadworth brewery. Gerald, brought up at Longworth Hall, had moved to Brenda's family home, Breinton Court, after their marriage two years earlier. 'I can't keep wishing

I was with you just to do little things for you,' he wrote on his way to the front. Lea was killed by shell shrapnel on 15 September.

The deaths marked a succession of tragedies that, for the next four years, would visit local families such as that of Hereford solicitor Loder-Symonds. Commander Frederick Parland Loder-Symonds, mentioned at the start of the chapter, was one of their eight children and destined to be the only male survivor: John, a former Hereford Cathedral School pupil, died that November at Ypres; Robert was killed in action the following March; Thomas was killed in May, 1915 and William in 1918. Their mother died of despair in 1917. A year later her daughter May was drowned when her ship, the *SS Galway Castle*, was attacked and sunk by a German U-boat in September. As former Hereford Valuation officer, Pte C.H. Lewis with the British Expeditionary Force put it in a letter home: 'England will never know. It's hell absolutely.'

Studio portraits such as this one of a soldier is his winter coat were a constant comfort to those at home. Uncensored letters from the front, however, began to convey the horrors of war.
(Photo: Herefordshire Museum Service)

On 5 December 150 men from the Hereford Regiment departed on the 9.35am train for Northampton, having marched with full ceremony from the Drill Hall past the Lord Scudamore School and through the town. They sang songs such as *It's a Long Way to Tipperary* as they marched, their departure causing many tearful good-byes at the station. The month turned out to herald the wettest Christmas in three years. The weather and a growing shortage of roadmen to carry out essential hedging and ditching saw the condition of the country roads worsen. The year drew to a close with some unseemly municipal bickering on another matter. City Councillor Langford complained about the purchase of flower bulbs for planting in Castle Green. The bulbs had cost £10 from Kings Acre Nurseries. What, he demanded to know, had happened to last year's bulbs? Alderman Wallis brushed the query aside. 1915, he predicted, would be a year of victory and great rejoicing, and they would want all the flowers and colour they could find. It was not to be.

Chapter 3

1915

Six months into the war the prevailing mood was one of gloom and bitterness. Housewives were gloomy about the soaring prices and the growing casualty lists; soldiers were bitter about the men who remained at home. Anyone could see that war would not end any time soon.

On May Day in Kington, the townspeople were determined to make the most of their bank holiday. A carnival procession and party were organised, ostensibly to raise funds for the poor Belgians, but mostly to have a good time. There were floats depicting patriotic tableaux including one staging a replica of a blitzed Belgian house. The May Queen, Nony Thomas, accompanied by pages Cyril Hicks and Harry Pennell and ladies-in-waiting Lalla Stevenson and Madge Mitchell, rode in a cart behind the 2nd Hereford Regiment Band and the drums and fifes of Kington's council school. Schoolchildren rattled their collecting boxes under the noses of passers-by and butcher H.J. Oliver tethered a live pig in his doorway, charging revellers a fee to guess what would be its dead weight. When the animal was slaughtered that evening it tipped the scales at 151.75lbs. Five winners shared the prize, but by now the day was spoiled.

During the morning procession a dray, mounted with a cannon and led by farm bailiff William Preece, had hit the parapet of the town bridge when its shire horse took fright and backed up. Ten-year-old Elsie Jones, the daughter of the landlord of the Bridge Inn, had been crushed and died in the arms of an onlooker. Hundreds were perishing on the front, but the accident involving little Elsie seemed to cast a deeper shadow over the community. The death of the poet Rupert Brooke, a regular visitor to Ledbury, a few days earlier, went unrecorded locally.

In 1914 Brooke had spent many evenings with fellow poets Edward Thomas and Wilfrid Gibson at Gibson's home, The Old Nail Shop, on the Herefordshire border near Dymock. Before he departed for war as a member of the British Mediterranean Expeditionary Force that February Brooke recalled a blaze of poppies he had seen in the neighbouring fields. 'I shall always remember them,' he told his friend Catherine Abercrombie. The flowers would come to symbolise the war's dead and Brooke's poem *The Soldier* would become an anthem of the time:

If I should die think only this of me
That there's some corner of a foreign field
That is for ever England.

The home fields, meanwhile, were being scrutinised by the farming community. Their assessment was downbeat. Mr Thompson at the Hyde told the *Hereford Times*: 'We are entering upon the year under anything but normal conditions, this county being in the throes of the greatest war the world has ever experienced. And no one can foresee the end.'

Labour was scarce and pay had risen – not high enough, declared Sidney Box, blaming the labour shortage on the low wages paid by farmers. In March Box held a union meeting at the Axe and Cleaver in Much Birch, but with 16 local members 'gone to the army' it was poorly attended. Box reported that at nearby Bishopston only six farm labourers were left out of 49 at the start of the war. Across the county, he declared, 500 Workers' Union men had enlisted.

Fertilizer was dearer, feeding stuff was up by nearly 30% and potash salts had doubled in price. At least one pedigree herd dealer, J.G. Cooke-Hill of Shelsley (he was also a Worcester Justice of the Peace) had been declared bankrupt with debts of £130,000. (Later in the year, the announcement that he had died prompted widow Mrs Powis, formerly of Floodgates Farm near Pencombe, to expose Cooke-Hill for embezzling some compensation money she had received. The landlord of the Falcon at Bromyard was puzzled: 'We all had confidence in him. If he'd a come to me the day before he disappeared and said: "Can you let me have £50 cash?" I'd have given it to him like a shot' although, he added ruefully, 'there's 26 solid sovereigns I'll never see again.')

On a more positive note farmer Thompson foresaw better produce prices and higher demand for livestock from abroad 'at the end of this terrible war'. Exports of pedigree calves would continue through the war, Brampton Bryan's L.L. Moore, H.R. Hall of Ashton, Leominster and J.R. Hill of Orleton all shipping stock to South Africa out of London's East India Dock during 1915. Hop growers were worried about government predictions of a 35% fall in beer consumption (several hop farmers were reported to be considering diversifying into cheese production), but in Leominster, at least, people were drinking as much as before. That July the licensing authority called Thomas Fudger, licensee of the Crown and Sceptre, before them after police opposed the renewal of his licence. The police were concerned that, while Fudger ran a respectable house, there were five more pubs including the Hop Pole, Anchor, Gold Lion and Bird in Hand close by. Fudger accounted for his annual orders: in 1913 – 80 barrels of beer, 686 dozen bottles of beer and stout and 35 gallons of wine and spirits; in 1914 – 73 barrels, 1,075 dozen bottles and 38 gallons of wines and spirits. He was allowed to keep his licence.

The Clehonger cider maker, A.E. Ridler, was also selling more white cider wine, partly because of supply problems with wine from France and partly because of the increased demand from patriotic squires who wanted nothing more to do with any foreign wines. But cider, unless it was used to drown the farmers' sorrows, could not resolve the over-riding problem in agriculture: the shortage of men. Some farmers became demonstrably depressed: 43-year-old William Pritchard of Eardisley was bound over to keep the peace after trying to kill himself with his shotgun. The solution for A.P. Turner, who farmed at The Fayre Oaks, Hereford, was that farmers invest in labour-saving devices such as double-furrow ploughs and lightweight cultivators. The county's Provincial Advisory Committee responded by arranging training courses in the use of these new machines.

Many Belgian refugees helped out on local farms and Mr H.A. Welch, manager of Hereford city's Labour Exchange, reminded the farming community that Belgians were permitted to work on farms where no English labour could be found. One newspaper pictured two families, the Luys and the Claeys, then living at Burghope Cottages as 'guests of Wellington parish'. The men, former railway and dock workers who had been neighbours in Ostend, were now employed by the county council 'on Dinmore road works'. Meanwhile the village school room remained a source of labour and, until his death that April, the Education Committee's Sir James Rankin continued to campaign against prosecuting parents who allowed their 12-year-old boys to do land work. Yet when Ledbury's School Attendance Committee advised against bringing several prosecutions of parents for allowing the irregular attendance of their children, the committee was criticised by the county Education Committee for interfering with the proper business of the magistrates.

Six months into the war the local press still portrayed a county going about its business as usual: there were advertisements from London's Goldsmith College seeking men and women students, from Malvern College Preparatory School looking for new boys and the Broomy Hill Academy in Breinton Road – 'an up-to-date commercial school' under Charles E. Holt – touting for business. Mr R. Beaven at the Canal Wharf in Hereford was advertising for a hurdle maker ('constant employment'); the Bage at Dorstone needed a cowman and Miss Decie of Bircher, Tenbury sought a boy to live in ('strong girl may apply').

In May bathers began their customary river swimming once again, the Wye in a 'splendid condition, being both fresh and of a comfortable temperature,' according to the *Hereford Times*. 'The advent of summer weather saw bathing commenced at

Bathers at the Bassom, the municipal swimming station on the river Wye at Bartonsham, regularly enjoyed the company of men from the RAMC taking their morning swim.
(Photo: Herefordshire Libraries)

the Bartonsham Bathing Station, maintained by the Town Council, being opened on Tuesday.' City people made their way over Wyeside Meadow, (later the Bishop's Meadow; it had recently been gifted to the townspeople on a 999-year lease by the Church Commissioners) and crossed the Victoria Bridge to Bartonsham. In its first week of the season the station tempted 369 bathers 'including 30 ladies on Thursday afternoon' into the water. The usual custodian was away on military service, leaving PC F. Bromage, the nephew of former attendant, Reuben Bromage, on river watch with Tom Preece 'in charge of the boat'.

The bathers, however, were now sharing their venue with a host of young men in khaki: 'Every morning the swimming members of the Royal Army Medical Corps in training at the Barracks, parade for a river bathe, and at least 50 enjoy the matutinal plunge at the Bartonsham,' reported the newspaper.

War was coming closer and a sudden bout of summer storms seemed to signal the change. In July a cyclone stripped the hops from the bines at Mr W. Griffiths' Alders End hopyard causing thousands of pounds of damage. Several people reported hearing the distant gunfire from France and there were more widows than the year before. At the sound of the telegram boy's bell, families with men on the front braced themselves for bad news: 'We regret to inform you …'.

As the 2nd Battalion Hereford Regiment returned to Northampton from training in Essex, and with the harvest looming, the farm labouring situation was becoming critical: 'The agricultural labourers have responded to the call to arms in such numbers that in many districts farmers are with staffs which cannot possibly do the work that is required,' warned the *Hereford Times*. (One homesick English family wrote to the newspaper from Canada offering to undertake harvest work for any farmer who would pay their passage home. The man and his two sons promised to pay back the loan of passage money with a '5% interest on outlay'.)

Farmers' leaders were reluctant to use prisoners of war ('the work of guarding them would be difficult,' explained a spokesman) or women ('voluntary work is all very well, but the work is hard, and it must be done without break,' warned another). Instead they seized on a War Office offer of soldiers from the Hereford Regiment, RAMC, ASC and KSLI on a 14-day furlough. The relevant forms, made available at the Hereford Labour Exchange, outlined the farmers' responsibilities: the farmers were to collect and return the soldiers at the railway station, (the government saw to their rail fares) and pay them 4 shillings a day, or 2½s with lodgings, 'wet and fine days whether they worked or not'.

The streets were starting to fill with men in khaki, prompting one Moorfields man, discharged as medically unfit, to appeal to be allowed to wear a special badge 'or the noble khaki' until the war was over if only to stop the constant badgering of recruiting agents. The Dean of Hereford, meanwhile, encouraged the ladies of Herefordshire to be more 'energetic' in presenting non-enlisted men with the coward's white feather. The Moorfields man's request promised to be met when, in December, it was announced that men who had enlisted, together with non-commissioned officers and men who had been discharged from the forces on medical grounds ('with a character not less than good'), would be entitled to wear a khaki serge armlet decorated with a crown picked out in red stitching. It was also hoped that the armlets would reduce the incidents of over-eager

The James family worked the tenanted Marsh Farm at Upton Bishop before the war. After his father and one brother died and his second brother emigrated to Canada, Alfred James was left to manage the farm alone. The young man felt compelled to enlist when a woman at Ross market thrust a white feather into his hand. (Photo: Keith James)

women giving the feather to men who, through no fault of their own, could not enlist. As one recipient put it, women should approach 'only bona fide slackers. How would innocent ladies like to be handed a badge branding them with some terrible conduct?' he wondered.

In Ross, meanwhile, Alfred James of Marsh Farm, Upton Bishop suffered the humiliation of being handed a white feather by a woman at the market. James strode off burning with shame. After the death of his father and brother he had been managing the tenanted farm alone and managing to make it pay. James was a prize-winning former pupil at Upton Bishop school and respected for diligently ringing the bell in church every Sunday. The white feather was too much to bear. Believing, as most young men did, that he would survive, that the war would be over soon and that he could return to put the farm in order, he enlisted. The next time he was seen at market he was wearing the uniform of the Royal Garrison Artillery.

Not all uniforms were British khaki. Joseph Marichal wore the blue-grey of the French army when in town. He, his wife Jessie and their children, Eve, Phyllis and Maurice had been among the 763 survivors of the luxury Cunard liner *Lusitania*, sunk by a German submarine off the coast of Ireland that May. During the rescue Jessie lost the child she was expecting and former Hereford United goalkeeper Allan Dredge and his wife were among the 1,198 who drowned. The Marichals moved to Hereford, Joseph suspecting that he had become the victim of a smear campaign after he told the official inquiry into the sinking that he thought the *Lusitania* was carrying munitions. (The sinking of the ship became a major factor in drawing the Americans into the war three years later.) Jessie would be widowed the following August when Joseph was killed at the Somme fighting alongside his French comrades.

By now the customary 4.05 train from Cardiff to Hereford had come to be known as the wounded train. In early June it arrived with 20 new casualties aboard. The men were sent to Hereford Hospital to occupy beds only recently vacated by a batch of wounded soldiers who had arrived in February and May. Aside from one Herefordshire man, Pte Worrell of the First Royal Rifles, who was said to be still nursing an obstinate bullet wound, the others had been sent back to the front line. By now the VAD wards at Hampton Grange were full of convalescing soldiers although those with less serious injuries were given therapeutic drives around the countryside in cars loaned by ladies, noted the local press, such as Mrs Blackwell, Miss Lea, Miss Hopton of Holmer and Mrs Ramsden. Other ladies including Mrs Spurway from Bridge Street, Hereford, Lady Ada Croft and Mrs Higgins of

Jessie Wadworth of Breinton Court, one of the many wealthy women who promptly volunteered to help with war work. (Photo: Hereford Archive and Records Centre)

Fownhope sent along gifts of magazines, eggs, rhubarb, rabbits and lettuce. None, however, quite matched the determination of Kington's Mrs H.H. Bromfield, who had succeeded in collecting 4,500 hens' eggs which were delivered to Kington police station to be sent to a central depot for wounded soldiers and sailors.

Most ladies, and many gentlemen, were involved in fundraising. Nellie Greenland, Hereford's mayoress, started a Hereford ambulance fund while Mr L.M. Duncombe of The Cloisters, Hereford raised £62 for the Blue Cross Fund for injured horses, which, he pointed out, made no distinction as to nationalities of the animals. Collections were made at the Castle Green every Sunday from audiences listening to the military band concerts. (With strict laws governing Sunday trading there was little else to do on the Sabbath: in August Hereford city sweet shop owner, Quarter Master Sergeant M.C. Oatfield, was fined for allowing his shop to open on a Sunday.)

The military bands were employed to encourage more men to enlist and Alfred Watkins from the Hereford Recruiting Committee wrote to the newspapers to insist:

Ledbury Volunteer Band. Local bandsmen regularly performed in public.
The sound of martial music in country town squares and on the Castle Green at Hereford
was considered a useful recruiting tool by Alfred Watkins.
(Photo: Herefordshire Libraries)

Recruits also formed bands to entertain the troops whilst in camps in the county.
(Photo: Herefordshire Museum Service)

A Mr Lloyd speaking at a recruiting meeting at Mortimers Cross in 1915,
(Photograph by Alfred Watkins, courtesy of Herefordshire Libraries)

Military manoeuvres such as this one at Painscastle were now a regular feature of country life,
and often closely observed.
(Photograph by Alfred Watkins, courtesy of Herefordshire Libraries)

Herefordshire volunteers fete at Vineyard Croft, the home of Alfred Watkins, in 1915.
(Photograph by Alfred Watkins, courtesy of Herefordshire Libraries)

'Our experience is that [the military bands] most certainly add to the numbers of recruits joining.'

The figure of Watkins in his grey flannel Harris Tweed was as familiar a sight in the city as his name was in the newspaper columns, both as a letter writer and the author of the latest transactions of the local natural historians' Woolhope Club. A self-educated polymath, Watkins became Tupsley's county councillor in 1914 and subsequently involved himself in almost 100 recruitment meetings. Traditionally a Liberal, he was set to become the military representative on the Hereford Recruiting Tribunal. He also served as a magistrate, the pool of available magistrates having been diminished by the deaths of Rankin, Judge Lea who died that May (his death, it was said, hastened by that of his son Gerald) and Lt William Kevill-Davies of Croft Castle, killed at Ypres on May 15.

In August a curious celebration took place at the Hereford Shirehall when around 2,000 people marked the anniversary of the declaration of war. Pianist Percy Heins was joined by singers Miss Haden, William Batey from the cathedral and a Mr Jones. The city's chief steward and former MP, John Arkwright of Kinsham Court, invoked Hereford's most famous freeman, Lord Nelson, for the fight ahead. The current MP, William Hewins, meanwhile, claimed that 'our resources, strength and powers for striking for the right are incalculable. Do we want to see women outraged, children killed, churches desecrated, altars brought down, institutions destroyed and trades ruined as in Belgium, parts of France and Poland?' he demanded, moving the resolution,

unanimously adopted, that the city of Hereford 'records once more its inflexible determination to continue to a victorious end'.

Similar patriotic sentiments were displayed by Ledbury magistrates later that month
when they considered a charge against the Girls' County School headmistress Clara
Creasey, accused of hitting a 12-year-old pupil, Dorothy Davies. The prospects for Miss
Creasey (she had been appointed during the 1913 teachers' strike) did not look hopeful.
One magistrate, Mr A. Carless, had declared an interest (the teacher had punished two
of his own children) and stood down. There was compelling evidence of injuries from
Dorothy Davies' doctor. But the case was dismissed after Miss Creasey explained that
her lesson that day was on the war and its anniversary, an important lesson that had been
disrupted by the unruly girl.

Summary justice with a cane or the back of the hand was a matter of course for most
children. More serious crimes were met with more serious measures. At the Hereford
Children's Court in June two shoplifters, 9-year-old Ivor Lloyd and 8-year-old Willy
Clarke, both of Millbrook Street, were sent to industrial school until their 16th birth-
days. A case against young William Davies of Green Street, whose father was on military duties and his mother at work, was adjourned, while 12-year-old Alfie King was
sent to a training ship: he had stolen, and tried to pawn, a pair of children's slippers.
His father told the court that since he started work as a carter at 5.30 every morning
he could not keep an eye on his boys. He was ordered to pay 1 shilling a week towards
Alfie's maintenance. Two Monmouth boys, aged 13 and 9, caught stealing food, toys and
cutlery from the Great Western Railway were sentenced to be birched.

The boys would have had a better time in the Scouts. In April the Lugwardine troop
displayed their physical drill and signalling under Scoutmaster George Dalby and by
mid-May were marching out to check the telegraph lines and guard the railway bridge
at Withington as the troop trains passed. The Scouts were trained to look for saboteurs
although it was reservists who arrested a man, deaf to their challenges, when he was
spotted acting suspiciously near the Ashford rail bridge over the river Teme. With bayonets fixed the Reserve marched him to Ludlow police station where he was identified as
'old Mr Milstome', a deaf local fisherman. The Reserve were met with ironic cheers from
passers-by when Mr Milstome was released from custody.

The extra traffic on the railways caused a corresponding increase in accidents: driver
Ernest Williams was lucky to survive when his goods train hit the barriers at the north
end of Ledbury tunnel, overturning and pinning him to the ground. Ernest Terrett of
49 Foley Street, Hereford was not so fortunate. He died after falling beneath the rolling
coal wagon he was working on at Risca in the Welsh Valleys. Incidents such as these
did nothing to improve the mood of local railwaymen, who had met in March at the
Hereford Picture House to discuss demands from their unions, the National Union of
Railwaymen and the Associated Society of Locomotive Engineers and Firemen, for
higher wages. They decided against pressing for a strike and instead passed a motion
demanding a 5 shilling a week increase and agreeing to lobby for more labour representation on the town council.

Meanwhile the prospect that Britain might lose the war and be invaded by the
Germans persuaded some to arm themselves with one of the three guinea Martini rifles,

then on sale at Seal Bros at 63 Eign Street, Hereford: 'War – Everyone Be Prepared,' warned Seals. Anything associated with Germany was bitterly resented. In August steeplejacks climbed the tower on Hereford Town Hall and removed the heraldic eagle, a symbol of Germany. It was mockingly rumoured to have been ceremonially drowned by Boy Scouts. Another rumour began to circulate that earnest ecclesiastical discussions were taking place over the plumage – Germanic or British? – of the heraldic eagle in the nave of the cathedral.

At Elton's Marsh, Burghill, neighbours Kate Butcher and Mrs Fosbrook fell out when the former's daughter called Mrs Fosbrook a 'German'. The case was brought to court and Butcher found guilty of assault and fined 7½ shillings although it was said in her defence: 'Very often women who had given their husbands to fight for their country [as Mrs Butcher had done] were left alone in a very precarious position. Any woman with a vicious tongue could make their lives unbearable.' But why call Mrs Fosbrook a German, enquired a bemused magistrate? The daughter in question replied candidly: 'Well, they are like Germans when they quarrel.'

In Monmouth members of the Poor Law Guardians wanted to know why two sisters, married to Germans now interned, and living at the workhouse received more aid than the other female paupers. Chairman S.J. Elson had to explain that the women's money, in one case 9½ shillings a week, was paid not by the Guardians, but by an American charitable committee.

Adolphus Wetters, the former Allensmore headmaster now teaching at Bromyard, was once again in deep water over his own alleged allegiance to Germany. He was moved once again, this time to Peterchurch, but fared no better there. He took lodgings at Hinton Farm and rashly shared his views on the war with the farm's Miss Holland. England, he told her, ought never to have entered into war. It was time to sue for peace and leave France to make its own terms. Alarmed by such unpatriotic sentiments Miss Holland, who happened to be the vicar's sister, passed Wetters' indiscretions on to her brother, who immediately telegrammed the education authority. They responded by dismissing him. Once more the unfortunate Adolphus Wetters found himself without a job.

It was difficult to get by even with a job. As the county council and Board of Agriculture set up a county agricultural war committee to look into ways of increasing food production, the prices of just about everything rose inexorably. The absentee owner of Whitney Toll Bridge had started charging disgruntled motorists an additional 6d per car on top of the 1d rate for each occupant. In Wellington grocers Edwin and Albert Price, owners of the Central Stores, declared themselves bankrupt with debts of over £800 which they blamed on war-related rising stock prices.

But the real victims of the war, according to inveterate letter writer C.C. Cooke of Much Marcle, were the wife and latest baby of the average labourer. They faced a weekly shopping bill of 17s 10d, which had risen from 11s 11d at the start of the war. By June, calculated Mr Cooke, prices had increased, in Much Marcle at least, by 34% since the outbreak of war. Shops reduced their opening hours, as the manager of Hereford Co-operative explained, so that employees would have to work no more than 48 hours a week. Consequently the Co-op closed its doors at 7pm instead of 8pm on Wednesday nights and half an hour early (9.30pm) on Saturdays. This seriously inconvenienced the wives of working men, who traditionally received their week's pay at 6pm on Saturday and often had a long walk home in front of them. There was a simple solution, suggested one exasperated letter writer to the newspapers: pay the men on Friday night.

One weight on the public purse was diminishing however: the cost of keeping the poor. The Hereford Guardians reported an unexplained decrease in expenditure of £1,173 in 1914 (the cost in 1913 had amounted to £11,235), but impoverished people continued to look for ways to make ends meet. Young lads regularly raided the nests of wild ducks, divvies (small ducks) and moorhens for edible eggs at Holmer's old gravel pits until, on 5 May, two brothers from Hopbine Terrace were drowned trying to fetch eggs from one of the islands. Ten-year-old Walter Smith perished trying to save his 8-year-old brother, Gilbert. As in Kington, infant deaths struck at the heart of country communities. There was common grieving at Sutton when two children died within weeks of each other, the 2-year-old son of waggoner Charles Price and the 4-year-old daughter of farm labourer John Vale who died after her dress caught fire. Allensmore, too, was struck by tragedy in May when five children, aged from 5 down to 3 months, died from dysentery contracted from polluted well water. In August 65-year-old John Walters, a villager close to the families, killed himself by cutting his throat. It was said at his inquest that he had been overcome with grief.

Some individuals managed to turn the war to their advantage. A judge sitting at Leominster was asked to order former horse slaughterer and now reservist, Robert Lewis, then stationed at Shrewsbury Internment Camp for German prisoners of war, to pay his outstanding debts. Witnesses claimed that Lewis had given his money to housekeeper Alice Parry who paid it in to Leominster's United Counties Bank to keep it away from his creditors. (The creditors included Lewis's former wife and the Revd J. D. Scott.) But Alice Parry who insisted that all the money was hers, assured the court: 'He is serving his King and country and would pay his account if he could.' The judge took no further action.

Entertaining the troops and keeping them out of the kind of mischief that might land them in the city Military Detention Barracks (it stood on the site of the old work-house gardens off Commercial Road) involved anything from the theatre and cinema to the curious 'hat trimming exercise' laid on that July at Hereford golf club and pictured in the local press. The YMCA was on hand to help: Abergavenny YMCA's organising secretary Gordon Griffiths appealed for bagatelle boards, books for competition prizes and 'whiffs' (cigarettes) in July for the 3rd Herefords camped near the town. Griffiths explained: 'Our talented friends have come to the rescue in the evening to entertain [the troops] with concerts and singsongs.'

That same month the Wye Valley Otter Hunt offered its own form of troop entertainment to the people of Ross. The RAMC had mounted a morale-raising march from Hereford to the market town under Lt-Col Herbert Jones. During their week-long camp in Ross the men organised a charity cricket match which raised £30 for the Red Cross. The match itself was a rarity: in May Tupsley cricket club secretary E.E. Morris had revealed that city clubs could no longer muster the necessary eleven players. The county sporting calendar was withering away. (As one newspaper correspondent put it, a young man in flannels carrying a racket was likely to cause an outcry in the 'present state of the public temper'.)

In Ross the RAMC continued to entertain the townspeople with demonstrations, bathing displays and a church parade. The visit concluded with a day's otter hunting at Wilton Bridge ('no find') and a glamorous riverside picnic with local ladies lining the bank, the men in khaki, huntsman Griff Davies afloat on the stream and refreshments laid on by Mr S.H. Deakin.

Despite the dearth of sporting fixtures, and despite rumblings of discontent, fox and otter hunting continued through the war. Col Clowes, one of hunting's foremost advocates, was knocked unconscious in March after being thrown from his horse while hunting at Dinmore. Assisted home by Docklow's Capt E.L.A. Heygate, Clowes recovered quickly. He fared better than the Herefordshire brakesman George Ord, killed three days later by the Abergavenny train at nearby Moreton-on-Lugg. Horseracing had also continued and at a spring meeting on Hereford race course the police nabbed professional gambler Henry Robins when they caught him operating the popular but illegal dice game 'Crown and Anchor'.

Given the state of the war, any form of public entertainment provoked considerable public debate, although the cancellation of the Hereford Rose Show prompted Mrs Clive, wife of the Ross MP, to call for its reinstatement. One traditional sport revived in late October was the starling shoot. Three hundred of what were described as 'strong birds' were released from five traps in front of guns at the Hereford racecourse. Sportsmen from Bristol, Birmingham and Cardiff competed at the kill and after the famous crack shot, Count Tres Antzini of Cardiff, stood down indisposed, a Mr Green from Bristol was announced the winner.

Earlier in the year a campaign had been launched to stop the Hereford May Fair. It prompted soldier W. Meredith, then with the British Expeditionary Force, to write in its defence (as did Alfred Watkins): 'It is the only enjoyment the poor people look forward to all the year round and we should not like to hear that they have been deprived of it.' The introduction of the Defence of the Realm Act or DORA ('We're under DORA now' was a well-worn joke) meant less extravagant lighting and the Fair having to shut earlier than usual. It did not prevent the odd moments of May Fair mayhem when, for example, irate farmer Edward Rees from Bridge Farm, Wellington, was involved in an altercation with an equally irate showman, resulting in Mr Rees being thrown from his cart. But there was one good reason for continuing the Fair: recruitment.

The previous October the *Hereford Times* Roll of Honour had run to four and a half pages and listed over 4,250 volunteer officers and men. However, enthusiasm for the war was on the wane and it drew the spectre of conscription closer, causing one local clergyman to caution against it: 'To force a man to do what he does not perceive to be his duty is oppression.'

Lady Evelyn Cotterell worried that 'in some cases [women] are withholding their menfolk from joining the Army … or at least not encouraging them to do so.' She revealed that the 1st Hereford Battalion could not proceed abroad until an additional reserve of 500 men had been formed. A letter writer signing himself 'Enlist Now' was less circumspect. The Battalion, he declared, was marooned by slackers. The fall-off in recruits was 'a disgrace to the county'. This encouraged another anonymous letter writer to reveal the whereabouts of these 'young men [who] hulk about the beer houses when the nation requires them elsewhere. They are to be found in the following places: Pembridge, Bearwood, Weston, Broxwood, The Meer, Sarnesfield, Titley, Almeley, Eardisley, Woonton, Weobley, Dilwyn and several farms in between. It is a disgraceful thing.' The letter elicited at least one angry response: 'The Meer, with the smallest population which numbers approximately 42, has sent 12 young Britons to serve King and Country.'

Yet, according to one recruiting officer quoted in the local press, Herefordshire farmers were 'the worst class in the county in terms of recruiting'. The charge led the Shropshire Farmers' Union to advocate a Herefordshire farmers' list, as they had done, of all the farmers' sons currently serving in the forces. The Workers' Union's Sidney Box added his own observation: 'I and others are anxiously awaiting for proof of the patriotism you give farmers credit for. Do they show it by enlisting, by taking into account the increased cost of living to their employees, or in the sale of produce or horses required by their country? Emphatically no.'

Sir John Cotterell continued to play a leading role in recruitment. He attended one recruitment rally at Burley Gate where, after the Revd H.G. Morgan promised to drive new recruits to Hereford in his car, five men stepped forward. But at Cradley, even after a lengthy appeal by Col Wood of the County Territorial Association, only a single recruit, Alfred Charles Taylor, offered his services. (Cradley had already sent between 60 and 70 men to the Front along with 24 from Mathon.) In May Mr F. Chambers of Hatfield Court, Leominster reported that 11 parish men had enlisted, and at a recruitment meeting at Puddleston, blacksmith William Williams from the Whyle and Mr A. George from Rock Cottage, Leysters both stepped forward. During the meeting Mr Gibson Dyson launched a personal attack on the local members of rifle clubs in Puddleston, Kimbolton and Hamnish for not enlisting. Stung by Dyson's remarks the rifle association later claimed that 65 of their 147 members were now serving with the colours.

Families vied with one another to send a full complement to the front: Allensmore's parish clerk, Ben Taylor, had four sons, James, John, Leonard and Ben (who was killed in action in 1917) at the front. Mr and Mrs James Lea of River View, Upper Breinton sent five, Mr and Mrs Shock of Wood View Lane, Ross sent six and their fellow townspeople Mr and Mrs C. Lerigo of North Road, Ross sent five. Hereford police proudly sent another 13, one of them Constable George Pritchard who in 1911 had been pictured in full ceremonial uniform, mounted on his horse outside the Bishop's Palace. He died in action in 1917 and was awarded the Military Cross for bravery.

Villages were encouraged to compete in these patriotic stakes, spurred on when the *Hereford Times* published a list of parishes together with their populations and the number of volunteers. These included Bodenham (46 out of 735), Clifford (20 out of 747), Eardisley (27 out of 746), Linton (13 out of 738), Monnington (5 out of 75), Edwyn Ralph (2 out of 79) and Brobury (4 out of 54).

Such numbers fell short of the level of recruitment of young men who enjoyed the May Fair at Hereford that year. Recruiting officers had erected a tent emblazoned with the banner 'Book Here for Constantinople and Berlin' and, after enjoying the giddy excitement of the roundabouts and rides, 130 young men signed up. They came from far and wide – Thomas Bird from Llancloudy, William Preece from Staunton, Sam Woolas from Newtown, Leominster and Charles Evans from Westhope, amongst them.

Not everyone, however, was happy with this method of recruitment and clothier Stanley Powell, of 16 Widemarsh Street, mounted his own one-man protest in High Town. Handing out bills headed 'Socialists of Europe Require Peace', he stood his ground beside a poster that read:

May Fair 1915
Don't Enlist Until You Have Thought It Well Through
We Can Help You
Hereford Branch Independent Labour Party

A woman passer-by complained to one of the uniformed recruitment officers, who attempted to take the poster down. There was a scuffle and by the end of the month Powell was standing in the dock of the magistrates' court pleading not guilty to a charge of prejudicing recruitment under the Defence of the Realm Act. With Mayor Greenland in the chair flanked by R.L. Bamford, G.J. Caldwell and Alderman E.L. Wallis (Wallis' two sons were serving on the front) he could not have expected a sympathetic hearing. Instead he used his court appearance to make his feelings known to a wider public. 'It seemed clear to me that the young fellows during the May Fair were not being given a fair chance of considering their position,' he told the magistrates. 'A young man can be got on the spur of the moment to do things which, if he thought, he would probably not do.'

Powell conducted his own defence and as the case went on, it appeared that the recruitment officer had punched the young clothier to the ground and roughed him up. The clothier refused to answer further questions on the grounds that he might incriminate himself. In what would sound like a brave and moving speech a century later, but now elicited catcalls from the public benches of 'You ought to be ashamed!' and 'Why don't you go?', Powell went on: 'We shall never crush German militarism … except by the spirit of love.' After being found guilty and fined £25 with £5 5s costs, the clothier was hustled out of court by a back door to avoid the baying crowd. It would not be Powell's last day in court.

During the Leominster May Fair which, according to the local newspapers, was notable for its lack of 'the sterner sex', recruiting officers signed up another 29 young men without any interference from socialists. (The newspapers also noted that Studt's Scenic Railway donated an hour's takings to the Serbian Red Cross.)

As the number of volunteers for the 1st Battalion Reserve rose to 250, the county Education Committee became entangled in an unseemly wrangle over the enlistment of teachers. Several schools, with so many staff in the forces, were facing closure. (It prompted the Bishop of Hereford to offer the services of his clergymen as temporary teachers, an offer firmly refused by the committee.) Committee member E.H. Hopkins, belittling the sacrifice that many soldier teachers were prepared to make, criticised staff for enlisting and saddling the committee with understaffed schools.

The 'tempting offer of a half salary and the Army rate of pay' for teachers was, according to Hopkins, excessively generous. Mr H.J. Southall agreed. The authority, he claimed, was practically bribing teachers to go and he seconded a motion that 'in future schoolmasters and assistant schoolmasters should give notice before enlisting.'

Alderman Bulmer conjectured that many teachers had not enlisted because they feared that their jobs would not be kept open until they returned. This failed to satisfy Alderman James Corner. He gave the example of one local authority employee who was a magistrates' clerk currently in the army ('He's only a drill man'). He received a full salary of £375 a year plus his army salary of £635 and, as an official receiver, could earn another £300 to £400. He called on the education authority to be 'just before generous'. But Alderman Bulmer interjected: 'A man's motives [for enlisting] are known only between himself and his maker.' It marked a low point in the committee's deliberations and the motion was withdrawn.

Assisting the men to choose whether or not to enlist were the Anglican, Catholic and free churches. Some Christians, the Quakers included, pledged not to fight although leading Quaker Joseph Bevan Braithwaite junior supported the war. He was quoted in the national organ of the Quaker movement, *The Friend* which was printed in Leominster, thanking God that 'so many of our young men have enlisted … through [the] Friends Ambulance Unit, proving their peace principles are not mere loosely held opinion.'

Many clergymen left to become military chaplains. The Ledbury congregation were told of the departure of their rector, Revd F.W. Carney, for the front at the same time they learned of the death of local boy, Pte Harry Cooper, son of Robert Cooper of Orchardleigh Lodge, killed in Flanders. When Revd Cecil L. Money-Kyrle left Much Marcle to become an army chaplain his parish put on a parade of honour to Dymock railway station.

The Catholic congregations had been boosted by the arrival of the largely Catholic Belgian refugees, but Anglican attendances had been falling after a surge in 1914. Religious leaders responded by endeavouring to explain the war, Hereford Cathedral's new canon, Revd B.H. Streeter, offering a vague answer to the question, 'Why does God allow it?', during his first sermon. 'It is because for centuries the nations of Europe have followed ideals that are less than Christian; it is because of international commercial rivalries; and the tendency of one nation to look down upon and despise another; it is because of national oppression and national jealousies,' he told his congregation.

The Bishop of Worcester, however, demonstrated a distinct lack of Christian charity when he offered his views on government plans to give financial assistance to common-law wives if their 'paramour' was killed in action. 'When the authorities at first proposed to place the soldier's mistress on equal terms with the married wife a blow was threatened which would have injured the honourable estate of marriage.' The bishop did concede the need for legislation enabling 'fallen mothers' to claim from the state if their partner died in battle, but he declared himself no friend of such women and he attacked 'those girls who are likely to become mothers through the dangerous system of billeting of soldiers'. These 'cases of lust' were 'a slur on the thousands of clean minded soldiers' and should not be condoned simply because 'soldiers are soldiers'.

The *Hereford Times* backed the bishop, condemning the government's support for 'the unmarried wife' and warning: 'it would appear also to be most recommended to guard against indiscriminate granting of this allowance to immoral women'. At the same time the newspaper covered the story of Mrs Margaret Ashby Linford from Hill View, Ross, whose husband had left after their marriage in 1895, and who was forced to publicly petition the divorce court for the restitution of 'her conjugal rights'. Meanwhile Miss May Cotton of Tan Brook, Wellington was reported to have taken her former fiancé to court for breach of promise. A jury, hearing how he had confessed to 'popping out with a fresh girl', awarded her £25 damages.

If most male readers regarded such stories as frivolous but entertaining titbits, many women saw them as further examples of the male-dominated society in which they lived. No women were represented on the county council, Education Committee or neighbourhood recruiting panels, yet they were sending their sons and husbands to war and coping with the consequences when the men failed to return. But times were changing. Women were organising themselves and they were taking direct action. (There were some concerns expressed in the local press, for example, when Miss Mary Morton, the daughter of the vicar of Dinedor, left for Belgrade with the British Farmers' Unit 'to which agriculturalists in Hereford subscribed'.)

Women were beginning to feel more confident about expressing their views. At Hereford in March a 31-year-old woman, Lucy Carter, was sentenced to six-months' imprisonment for the manslaughter of her baby, but as Judge Mr Justice Avory passed sentence the wife of the assistant vicar choral at the cathedral, Ethel Davies, disrupted proceedings. She stood up in the public gallery and shouted at the judge: 'I protest as a woman and as a mother.' The judge ordered her from court. 'Take care that that woman is not admitted again,' he told the clerk. Ethel Davies was an ardent suffragette and she followed her courtroom interruption with a letter to the *Hereford Times* complaining about the absence of women in the judiciary and arguing that fathers were equally guilty and should be tried.

The clergy themselves were not immune to affairs of the heart as Abbeydore's parishioners were to discover. They were conjecturing on the hasty departure of their vicar, Revd M.E. Doorly, a quiet gentleman who had stood in for Revd P. Cave-Moyle. Cave-Moyle had left to become an army chaplain. Revd Doorly was in the habit of fetching the London newspapers from the early Pontrilas to Hay train. One morning in October, returning briefly to inform his hosts, Mr and Mrs Mason of The Schoolhouse, that he had pressing business in London, he departed on the Paddington train never to be seen in the village again. Later that month his wife Kate successfully petitioned him for divorce in the London courts on the grounds that he had several times 'misconducted himself with a coloured girl'.

By now local women were being encouraged to help in field and factory. Councillor Langford was already calling for more postmen to exchange their uniforms from King's to khaki since 'their work could easily be done by women until they returned' and by the end of June a Miss Powell was regularly to be seen carrying the mail from the Hereford post office to Barrs Court station where women had for some time been cleaning the coaches.

Dame Flora Steele, the popular author of all things Indian, joined women on a platform at Ludlow Town Hall to encourage more of her sisters to join in at the workplace. A Mrs Webster, however, pointed out that although there were plenty of 'healthy, strong young women' prepared to do field work, the pay was derisory. One local woman, she said, had been paid 1 shilling a day without food, another 10 pence. The problem according to Mrs Webster was not finding farmers willing to employ women; it was finding farmers prepared to pay a proper wage of at least 2 shillings a day. Mary Gwynne-Holford from Buckland Hall wrote to the local press to insist that 'much of the work on a farm can be done just as well by women as men. I don't say that they can do the same quantity of work in all cases but they can do it as well as men.' It prompted Hereford veterinary surgeon Hamilton Kirk to publish a list of 'lady helpers', women who had already volunteered for farm work, which included the Misses Ailsa and Marjorie Hatton of Mount Craig, Broomy Hill, the younger sisters of the artist Brian Hatton. Hatton had enlisted in the Worcestershire Yeomanry to serve in the cavalry and continued to sketch scenes of camp life including *Colonel Lutley's charger on a picket* (Lutley owned Brockhampton Court in north Herefordshire).

That spring the *Hereford Times* had published an extraordinary photograph: it showed a slightly built young woman ploughing with a pair of shire horses that towered above her. She was described as the daughter of 'a leading agriculturalist and pedigree Hereford cattle breeder in the Leominster district' and the picture caption carried the tortuous observation that 'many women have adapted themselves to various kinds of work on the farm'.

By mid-June women had set up a Farmers' Aid Women's Society. Mrs Underwood acted as chairman and Miss Maddison from the Hatton household acted as honorary secretary and treasurer. Mrs Leslie, Mrs Stanhope, Mrs Buchanan, Mrs Wilmot, Miss Underwood and Mrs Dickinson were listed as committee members, but the main movers were Mrs Bradstock of Yarkhill, Mr G.H. Bray of Dormington Court and Hereford vet Hamilton Kirk. The group called a meeting of 'women harvesters' at Hereford's Percival Hall and used the event to condemn the farming community's woeful ignorance of women's capabilities. Hop picking and bush and cider fruit gathering, for example, were regarded as well within the capabilities of 'ladies with no experience' but haymaking ('so much a matter of machinery') and horsemanship, which required 'experience of the leading and control of horses', was said to present significant difficulties for the fairer sex. So too were the demands of rising early and completing the job in hand. An ironic Mrs Dickinson suggested that parties of women could overcome such obstacles by working in relays.

Women, whatever their private feelings, were careful not to express support for a proposed peace congress, dismissed in the leader columns of the *Hereford Times* as a bunch of 'Peace Prattlers'. Instead the newspapers continued publishing letters from the front. They caused profound anxieties to anyone with a family member on active service. Pte G.H. Corbett wrote to his friend Mr E. Smith at Marden House, Hereford of how he had been gassed. 'I had a German helmet for you but when I was gassed I lost every-

City of Hereford.

POLICE NOTICE.

AIRCRAFT RAIDS

Defence of the Realm Regulations.

NOTE. The probability of an Aircraft Raid reaching Hereford is very remote, but in order to guard against this danger, however improbable, the following precautionary arrangements have been made :--

1. On notification by the Police of the approach of enemy Aircraft, a hooter will be sounded at the **ELECTRICITY WORKS, WIDEMARSH ST.,** which, in order to avoid confusion with Fire or other Signals, will give a series of very short blasts, with shorter intervals, to continue for about five minutes. No alarm must be sounded except by order of the Police, and persons causing unauthorised alarm to be sounded are liable to prosecution under the Defence of the Realm Regulations.

2. All persons, on hearing this signal, should at once get under cover. Their presence in the streets can be of no assistance and is only adding unnecessarily to their own risk of injury.

3. All external lights of every description must at once be extinguished; occupiers of houses, factories, and workshops, will be held responsible that, as far as possible, no light from inside is visible externally.

4. Police, Fire, and Ambulance Brigades will be called up, and held in readiness to give assistance if required.

FRANK RICHARDSON,
Chief Constable.

City Police Office,
   Hereford.
23rd February, 1915.

" Journal " Office, Hereford.

thing. It [being gassed] is just like being strangled or choked. You suffer agony. I wish everybody at home could see what it does to the boys and then they would all come out here. It is not war, it is pure murder.'

Driver A.W. Price was one of the four sons of Mr and Mrs Price of 34 Newmarket Street serving at the front. 'I am glad to say there are a lot of men from Hereford taking part – Jockey Bowen, Albert Smith, Jack Harrison, George Rivers, Bill Morris, Tom King, Bill and Fred Hancocks [Alfred Hancocks from Wall Street, Hereford would die in action in 1917] Cocker Webb and several others.'

In a letter to his parents, Mr and Mrs F. Preece of Highfield, Hafod Road, Hereford, Pte F.G. Preece of the London Rifle Brigade described the effects of a shell burst. 'Applin has a compound fracture, Mair a slight wound, Wheeler a bad scalp wound. Jimmy and Thomas are all right, but Tucker who was married only a few days before he came out, was killed. My friend Lintoff was also killed by a shell. That night we came away from a place I never thought to leave alive.'

The list of local casualties published in the newspapers was growing. Major C.A. Wilkinson from the Grange, Bishopswood, Ross and butler Sgt Haugh and groom Pte Rutherford, both employees of Colonel Hewat at The Elms, Aylestone Hill, had been reported wounded that May. Readers could also detect the raw horrors of trench warfare in the descriptions of the wounds: 'Pte. J. Howells, Richards Castle (shell wound in face), Pte H.J. Skyrme, Millbrook Street (gunshot wound in face)' and 'Pte J. Pocknell, Ferry Road, Fownhope (gunshot wound, neck)'. In the same weekend that 35-year-old William Hall lost his left arm in a threshing machine accident at Minster Farm, Much Birch, Pte James Thomas of the 2nd Battalion Worcestershire Regiment of 84 Bye Street, Ledbury, a former employee of Wilson's Florists, lost his right arm, smashed by a shell. He returned to live with his mother in Gaol Street, Hereford.

In mid-June, Cpl J. Valentine of the Dragoon Guards described, in a letter to his parents at No 5 Hotel, Widemarsh Street, being buried alive when a shell hit his trench. Yet he was upbeat about the future: 'The Germans knew they were fighting a losing game.'

Pte W. Eldridge from the 2nd Battalion Royal Welsh Fusiliers wrote to his former schoolmaster, Mr T. Adams from St Owen's council school of his 26 days in a trench, four feet deep, two feet wide and 400 yards from the German lines, 'wet through to the skin for days on end and continually standing in water' the previous November. Pte A. Sharpe from the 1st Battalion, now recovering in a Cambridge hospital, told his parents-in-law, Mr and Mrs Vaughan of Skenfrith, how, in the attack on Hill 60, he was hit in the stomach, arm and leg. 'There were heads, legs and arms flying in all directions. It was a terrible sight.'

Sapper William Gladwin of the Monmouth Royal Engineers, from Lower Road, Newton, Ledbury, told his father about a football match during a German air raid ('it did not stop the game') and of encountering a ghost town 'the size of Ledbury, and no one living in it, all the windows smashed and the walls blown in'. He ended: 'I notice in the paper that the boys of Ledbury have joined up well for the Army, and I shall be only too pleased to see any of them here. Still, I think there must be some that have not joined. Why don't they come along and do their little bit as well as us?'

By mid-summer an unfamiliar place name had started to appear in the newspapers: 'Lt Philip Bell, of Ledbury, gas poisoning and bombardier C.J. Bevan of Third Royal Artillery, (stepson of Mr F. Jones of The Firs, Ledbury) shot in head and lost an eye at the Dardanelles.'

To most Herefordians the Dardanelles were as distant as the Amazonian rainforest. A 60-mile strip of water dividing Europe from Asia, the Dardanelles and the Gallipoli peninsula were part of the Ottoman Empire and in the hands of another of Britain's wartime enemies, Turkey. With stalemate on the Western Front and the trenches blocking the overland route between England and France and their ally, Russia, military leaders saw the Dardanelles as an alternative sea route to Russia. However, a naval assault in February had failed to move the Turkish artillery on the peninsula protecting the straits. Consequently a land army, the Mediterranean Expeditionary Force, was assembled to take on the job. At the end of July the *Hereford Times* published a full list of 1st Herefords who would be serving there including 27 officers (Lt Col Drage, Maj Carless, Capts Yates, Green, Holman, Capel, Rogers, Archer Croft, Nott and Barker amongst them) and 967 men. Eventually 1,100 men from the Herefordshire Regiment would be sent out as part of the Allied force.

'Off we went to Gallipoli.' Pte Percy Pritchard survived the military disaster which killed so many Herefordshire soldiers. The photograph was taken whilst he was stationed in Egypt. (Photo: the Pritchard family)

Listed in that edition of the newspaper was Pte P. Pritchard (Number 2109) of 24 Broad Street, Hereford. The city tailor Percy Pritchard took up the story when he looked back on his life in the 1980s. 'Off we went to Gallipoli. I was in the landing at Suvla Bay. We had landed in tropical heat with a shortage of water and then came away in arctic conditions. I went through that six months.' It was a brief description of what would turn into a military disaster.

Gallipoli's 'great pest of existence' were the flies (John Cotterell appealed for mosquito and fly veils for the troops), although L.L. Thain from Ewyas Harold believed the real villains were the indigenous people. He wrote to the newspapers hoping that 'the numerous Jewish soldiers in the Allied Forces could be trusted to give a good account of the bloody Turks and Arabs and purge the land of such veritable Canaanites'. It was the Allies who faced defeat.

Capt Croft had been promoted to captain during the regimental training at Northampton and within days of sailing to Gallipoli in July he was reported missing. Only in mid-September was it revealed by his soldier servant, Pte William Oseman who had been wounded, that Croft had been brought down by Turkish snipers. Croft was carrying official papers strapped to his wrist when he and Oseman encountered

The son of a Hereford police constable, William Charles (centre left, pictured in Egypt) emigrated after seeing a story about Australia in his parish church magazine. Having worked on cattle stations he joined the Australian Imperial Force in April 1915 and found himself fighting alongside his former Hereford comrades in the Dardanelles. He died at Gallipoli. Five months later his older brother, Jim, enlisted in the Royal Field Artillery (far left, middle row in the photograph below). He survived the war only to be killed in 1923, shortly after becoming engaged, while decommissioning a faulty shell at Credenhill. (Photos: Judith Morgan)

intense machine gun fire as they tried to cross a lane. They ran into two stretcher bearers carrying a groaning man: 'Don't go down there; there are so many snipers about,' they warned, but Croft pressed on towards a well which was already littered with the bodies of British soldiers. Croft soon joined them.

'I felt as though I had lost a brother,' said Oseman later. At home in Lugwardine Court Lady Croft began opening her letters of condolences beside a photograph taken of her husband. Dressed in his uniform, he stood beside by their young son James similarly dressed in a matching soldier's uniform complete with Sam Browne belt, KSLI hat badge, puttees and boots.

Once again it was the soldiers' letters home that carried news of Gallipoli. A Bromyard boy who had emigrated to Melbourne and later joined the 6th Battalion Australian Field Force, Pte Neil Wells was injured during the landings. He wrote to his father at The Tan House: 'I got hit in the left arm, shrapnel. It knocked me out.' He died that July. A fellow Australian migrant and Herefordshire boy, William Charles had enlisted with C Company 18th Battalion Fifth Brigade Australian Imperial Force in April 1915. The 23-year-old was killed on August 27.

That December the letters carried reports of a terrible storm in Gallipoli. Accounts included that of Pte T.H. Isherwood to his father, Revd M.A. Isherwood at Orcop Rectory: 'The trench was flooded. We had to stick it for two days before we were relieved. Some of the men died in the snowstorm which followed. We had to sleep in the open on some rushes through the blizzard. Hundreds of men died from exposure. Seven Herefordshire men died in the Second Welsh troop.'

Percy Pritchard later recalled the 'terrific storm over Gallipoli [which] flooded all the trenches. Our regiment and rest of us, we were on our way down to the boats to embark, the Navy was taking us off. But they turned us out on what was the salt lake. It was an open expanse and we were all saturated and wet through and it froze in the night. There were hundreds of them all frozen through, some with their fingers dropping off, but the worst of it was the Indian mule convoys couldn't take the rations up the lines, they dumped them on the side of the track. And our fellows found the Jamaican rum. They poured it neat like treacle, just like that. Course in the morning they were stiff [dead].'

Evacuated from Gallipoli, Percy landed in Malta suffering from frostbite but, since all the English hospitals were full (of 1,100 men who returned, only 80 were fit enough to continue fighting), he was moved to an Indian hospital with 'Gurkhas and Sikhs and the Moslem. I had a most interesting time.'

But it was a black time for the people of Herefordshire as some 70 families received telegrams informing them of the deaths of their menfolk in Gallipoli. The telegrams would be followed by the commanding officer's letter, written in similar terms to this one sent to Robert Buchanan of Bosbury House, Ledbury after his son died on the front line in France:

> Dear Sir, I very much regret to let you know that your son Alan was killed in action on the morning of the 15inst. He was assisting to get a machine gun in position after our first advance to the front line of the German trenches, when he was hit in the head by a shell. His death was instantaneous, and he suffered no pain. He

was one of the bravest men we had, and when he was hit he was encouraging his comrades in the most cheerful way.

Alan Buchanan was 25.

A 27-year-old bandsman, Henry Harrison of the Ninth Lancers, had lived with his wife at Eign Cottages in Eign Road before the war. He was killed by a sniper on the Western Front. He was his mother's only son. 'I can assure you that your dear husband felt no pain when he was killed so unfortunately' read the officer's letter to his wife.

Such letters did little to encourage men to step forward and enlist. By November local recruitment was in freefall. Having peaked at 236 in April, October saw only 29 enlist. The county's casualty list, meanwhile, had topped 400. The government acted by bringing in the Derby Scheme, designed to test whether or not the forces' need for soldiers and sailors could still be met by volunteers. Lord Derby, the new Director General of Recruiting, required every man born between 1874 and 1897 and not in a starred or reserved occupation, to declare before a local recruiting committee whether or not he was prepared to attest to enlist. The deadline was set for 11 December and as plans were made to open a second recruiting office to cope with the expected rush, every man between the age of 18 and 41 was encouraged to collect his white card and a day's army pay of 2s 9d when he attested or risk ignominy and a white feather if he did not. In the event 291 single men and 259 married men stepped forward. (Locally and nationally the scheme was judged a failure: nationally over 50 per cent of married men refused to enlist. Conscription was inevitable.)

Those who attested were to be divided into age and marital groups. Single men would be called before the married men and those considering slipping off for a hasty wedding after the scheme started were warned that they would be considered single. VADS, Red Cross volunteers and special constables were reminded that they were not exempt and employers were told that 'nobody could exempt a man unless he went before the local tribunal after he had been duly attested and had his case considered impartially'. The promise of impartiality would be found wanting in the years ahead.

As Christmas approached Gunner W. West of Bromsash wrote to the *Hereford Times* with a particular plea: 'Please do not let anything stop or hinder the production of munitions. We shall want billions and billions of rounds and', he added thoughtfully, 'a box of Woodbines.'

The landscape that Gunner West had left behind was changing fast. Woodlands, especially, were disappearing to feed the demand for everything from pit props to trench works. Many venerable old trees were put to the axe. In 1915 the *Hereford Times* had published a photograph of the St Catherine's Oak being hauled from The Homend, Stretton Grandison by a steam traction engine as a correspondent wondered whether landowners were making the most of their old oaks. 'Owners of timber are making better prices than ever and therefore inclined to make hay while the sun shines,' he wrote. With seasoned Herefordshire oak fetching '6d per cubic foot per year', sums of £50 and even £70 had been offered for two fine specimens of English oak 'not many miles from Hereford' and the author suggested further 'steps may be taken to make better use of the splendid oaks which are dotted over our countryside'.

Chapter 4

1916

The start of 1916 was marked by violent storms which brought down one of the great elms that had sheltered Hereford Cathedral Close for centuries. As a consequence the cathedral authorities felled five of the leviathans that February, one of them injuring little Winnie Vale when she tried to run through the Close from her home in Church Street. 1916 would also see a swathe of Herefordshire men similarly brought down by war.

On New Year's Day Mrs Chadney of The Martins, Bosbury was expecting her husband home on leave. Instead she received a letter from Capt H.S. Collins of the KSLI: 'I am writing to sympathise with you on your poor husband's death. He was wounded in the trenches by a shell. I helped to dress him and I have seldom seen a man bear up so splendidly.' Staff at Kentchurch Court learned of the death in France of former worker Pte Tom Bull. L/Cpl W. Tyler of Grandstand Road was reported killed in the Mediterranean while Mrs Bridges of 46 Newmarket Street was left to bring up three children alone after her husband, 34-year-old Pte John Bridges, died from exposure. His brother, Albert Bridges of Gaol Street, had been killed only weeks before.

When in March Lieut Edward Hopton, the second son of the Hoptons of Homend and husband of Christabel Bourne of Cowarne Court, was reported to have died from pneumonia in Alexandria, L.L. Thain from Ewyas Harold warned in a letter to the papers: 'If this war should last another year farms will begin to be thrown up in thousands and go out of cultivation, big estates broken up from owners being unable to meet the enormous taxation. The same effect here has occurred during the French Revolution which ended in the disappearance of large land owners.' (Edward's elder brother Capt Guy Hopton had been killed the year before.)

Farming families struggled to manage as their sons went off to war. John Jones who, with his wife Annie, ran the farm at Wellington Court watched in dismay when their sons trooped off to war one by one. Bill and Sidney, engineers who had graduated from Cardiff University, joined the Royal Naval Reserves while Evan and Harold enlisted with the Lancers. At Gallipoli Evan and Harold would find themselves fighting side by side with their Herefordshire neighbours, Henry and Jim Patrick from the Nags Head at Canon Pyon. A fifth son, Rowland, was still at the Hereford High School for Boys, but with no one else to help on the farm his education came to an abrupt halt. He

Like many households, Wellington Court (above) supported a large family.
John and Annie Jones (right) had sons Evan, Harold, William and Roland
together with daughter Gladys to help on the farm. One by one they
volunteered until only Rowland remained. His time would come in 1918.

The Hereford Troop of the Shropshire Yeomanry (below),
with Evan Jones third from left in the back row.
(Photos: Barbara Perrin)

returned to work on the farm. (Bill, Sydney, Evan, Harold and the Patrick boys, Henry and Jim, would all survive their war service.)

The shortage of manpower on farms was more serious than ever. At a meeting of the South Herefordshire Farmers Society, Arthur Bellamy of Penallt, his son Robert away with the RAMC, asked after the cost of the new, 25 horsepower, horse-free tractor ploughs. At £445 they were expensive, but the Society agreed to club together to buy one. They set up a tractor co-operative with Mr Bell at Fawley, Mr P. Preece at Harewood End, F.C. Price at Bromsash, J.H. Sainsbury at Brampton and A.E. Rudge at Sellack. Yet when the Herefordshire War Agricultural Committee (HWAC) met, members were told of steam ploughs lying idle because of the lack of labour. Whole farms were rumoured to be standing empty and fields laid to grass. Hubert Reade from Walterstone suggested that Herefordshire follow the example of Devon WAC, which was considering importing labour from Denmark while committee member Philip Davies advocated recruiting more 'big burly boys and big, strapping wenches' to solve the problem. The Education Committee was already allowing schools to release children under 12 for farm work, but the perils of employing boys on the farm was brought home when 13-year-old Jack Stanley Harvey was killed at Lyde Cross Tree Farm, Munstone that April. The lad, employed by a Mr Patrick, had been run over by a cart.

There was confusion over the wartime role of farmers' sons: would they, like some of the essential farm labourers, be 'starred' and thus exempt from military service? The issue would be put to the test during the appeal tribunals later in the year.

In the meantime John Porter from HWAC appealed for farmers to shoulder a gun for a sustained attack on pigeons, crows and sparrows. Porter encouraged children to lay brick traps for sparrows and bring any dead birds, together with as many sparrows' eggs as they could find, to school, proposing that prizes be awarded to the most assiduous collectors.

His idea was met with derision. 'Surely the war has not brought us to such a pass as this?' asked a distressed Revd H. Somers Cocks of Eastnor Rectory. As the secretary of the Herefordshire Society for the Prevention of Cruelty to Animals he questioned whether children could discriminate between the house and the hedge sparrow and he worried that the children would kill other insectivorous birds that were acknowledged to be 'worth their weight in gold'. The national secretary of the Royal Society for the Protection of Birds, Linda Gardiner, weighed in to the argument, warning of an insect plague if too many wild birds were slaughtered. (That January local apiarists had already noted a serious drop in the bee population following the spread of a disease from the Isle of Wight.) Gardiner also pointed out that killing any wild birds during the breeding season, except by owners and occupiers of land or their agents, was illegal.

Meanwhile the Red Cross and Allies Relief Fund benefited from a fundraising auction at Hereford Market that January. Thanks to the gift of two pigs from Mr R.H. Hall of Holmer Grange, some sheep from cider maker Ridler at Clehonger and more pigs from Councillor E.W. Langford, Mr Rawlins Lowe of Dewchurch and Messrs J. and R. Edwards from Dewsall Court, £1,000 was raised. Capt Clive topped the fund with a gift of £100. At Ledbury a Red Cross donkey donated by Mr E.T. Lane of Old Court, Bosbury and Mr W.S. Lane of The Farm, Bosbury was sold and donated back at so many charity auctions that it too raised £1,000.

Farmers were accused of being less generous with their labourers' pay, which remained a bone of bitter contention. In mid-March a sudden fall of snow caught a woman from Hay Workhouse struggling to walk the few miles to Red House Farm at Cusop. She died in the attempt. The snowstorm also delayed the Board of Agriculture's Mr Allsebrook from reaching a farmers' meeting at Dore. When he finally reached them he delivered his hosts with a stiff lecture on the need for equality of work to be met with equality of pay. Herefordshire wages, he declared, had to be increased.

Returning to their labour problems, the South Herefordshire farmers heard complaints about the serious injury done by Lord Derby's Scheme. Meeting at the Imperial Hotel that spring, farmer Edward Rees from Wellington said indispensable men were being taken from the farms. He was backed by farmer W.E. Taylor who accused the local tribunals, which had begun hearing appeals from farm workers, of being biased towards the military. He supported a resolution for a letter of protest to be sent to the Board of Agriculture.

The following month Edward Rees, who had a son of his own in the army, attended the Hereford Rural Tribunal to observe its deliberations. Rees, who had been involved in the altercation with the May Fair showman the previous year, was backing the appeal of a young waggoner and ploughman, Henry Field. Rees said Field was needed because he, Rees, was trying to manage 400 acres at Bridge Farm, Wellington with another of his sons. The tribunal refused his request.

'Is it the duty of tribunals to strip farms of all labour?' burst out Rees. The Tribunal chairman W.G. Childs pointed out that, with 30 cases to consider, they had devoted 18 minutes to his case. 'We have tried to do our best,' he told Rees. 'Well you don't do it,' retorted the disgruntled farmer.

The first meeting of the tribunal had taken place on 26 February. It was headed by W.G. Bankes and included Mr T. Colbatch Clark, M.J.S. Swabey, Mr Childs, the cider man R.E. Ridler, J. Thorne, W.J. Andrews, H.J. Pewtress and Capt T.L. Morgan as the military representative. William Davies from Fownhope and W. Jones from Kington were nominated as labour representatives.

They allowed only a five-month exemption from military duties to the first two cases, a Westhide smallholder, F.W. Rowberry, and a small farmer from Tillington, Fred Patrick. There was a clash over Withington waggoner W.G. Smith. His boss, J.H. Yeoman, insisted that Smith was needed on the farm since he, Yeoman, had now lost six men to the forces. But Childs pointed out that a new motor plough had recently been acquired for the district: the waggoner was sent to war.

Other cases lost that day included that of Sutton farmer Robert Jancy and cowman R.F. Weaver from Ashgrove Farm, Marden. Also dispatched to the forces were stockman S.P. Harris of Tything Barn, Allensmore, gardener R. Nash of Belmont Cottages ('We don't want gardeners if we are sending farmers away,' explained Mr Banks) and Fred Goode, landlord of the New Inn at Fownhope, who warned that his pub would have to close. 'We are sorry but we have all got sacrifices to make in this wartime,' remarked the chairman, leaving the landlord musing on what sacrifices the tribunal members were making.

The Fownhope doctor, Dr Rae, was deprived of his chauffeur despite presenting the tribunal with his own medical evidence that the man in question, T.A. Jones, was unfit for service in the trenches. 'We will let the army decide', offered Capt Morgan.

Later in the year, amidst rumours that some single farmers had married hurriedly or taken a farm before the Derby Scheme came into play, Alfred James of Lily Hall, Gorsley strenuously denied trying to evade military service by temporarily increasing his farm stock. Nevertheless exemptions were granted to Christopher Godsell of Eggleton, who had recently left the employment of Mr Hawkins at Thinghill to run his own farm, and to H. Morris of Miles Higgins, Much Dewchurch. Cowman Thomas Jones of Larport was exempted until April when the cows would be turned out.

Also exempted temporarily was the South Herefordshire Fox Hounds' hunt groom and second horseman Len Andrews in order to give the Master, Capt R.W.B. Ker, time to find a replacement. It caused more mutterings of dissent that the hunts should continue to meet. Earlier in 1916 the secretary of the hunt, Dudley Smith of South Bank House, justified the need to hunt, publishing a letter from the director of Remounts at the War Office. The director had urged that hunting carry on 'for the continuance of breeding and raising light horses for cavalry work'. The director also recommended that men of military age who were indispensable to the hunts, should, as Capt Ker had done, appeal to the local tribunals. (Later, in September, the Earl of Harrington was quoted in the Herefordshire press warning that if fox hunting was abolished many rich people would leave the country in winter and spend their money elsewhere.)

Certain timber fallers were exempted. Masterman faller Sydney Watkins of Little Birch and William Weaver of Checkley Bush were exempted on the condition that they continue supplying pit wood (props), but another faller from Much Birch lost his appeal when the tribunal learned that he had a brother of working age. (The decimation of Herefordshire's woods was worrying to some: in June F.G. Carver wrote to the local newspapers from his home in Hounslow pleading that Dinedor's historic woods be saved from the woodsman's axe.)

There were similar scenes in the boardroom of Ledbury's Workhouse where the Leominster Rural Tribunal met. G. Butters, T. Edwards, J.M.P. Cave, H. Langford and R.H. George sat under the chairmanship of Mr J. Bazley with John Hughes as labour representative and Col J.E.R Campbell representing the military. The tribunal allowed temporary exemption to 19-year-old Nigel E. Bebb of Pulpits Farm, Little Hereford, but gave absolute exemption to Mark Poyner of Maund Farm, Bodenham on the grounds that he was the only man on 55 acres and was managing for his mother. The tribunal turned down shepherd and cowman Thomas James Holland of Broad Green, Orleton, corn dealer Albert Sydney James from Orleton Post Office and odd-job man and carpenter Robert Henry Cooke from the Portway, Leysters. Cooke told the tribunal he wished only to sell his sheep before enlisting.

On its first day Leominster Urban Tribunal allowed only two absolute exemptions in the 18 cases heard. The losers included parcel delivery man Henry Parker of Bridge Street and Frank Williams, a corn merchant with G.F. Hinton, waggoner T.E. James from Broad Farm, boot maker Thomas Pugh from 34 High Street and painter Roland Davies from Corn Square.

The *Hereford Times*, reporting on the early Hereford City Tribunals, fought shy of naming the appellants. Instead they reported that, under Chairman Mayor Greenland and military representative Col Hewat, the tribunal had thrown out the case of a chauffeur who had failed to find a woman driver to take his place; a sculptor who appealed on behalf of his son; a laundry owner who told the tribunal she could not manage the heavy work without her son; and a hairdresser who wanted time to sell his business.

By March appellants were being named and shamed. They included Stanley George Powell, who had been brought before city magistrates after the fracas at the May Fair the year before. Dressed in a sober grey suit, the 22-year-old stood before the tribunal and with his customary directness told them: 'I am a Socialist, believing in the brotherhood of man. I stand for two things: the abolition of the private ownership of land and capital; and the acknowledgement of love as the supreme power in the world for individual and social redemption.'

Col Hewat remarked that Powell's objections seemed to be political rather than religious. Alderman Jones asked irritably: 'If your country was attacked would you fight to defend your country or your home?'

'I take it that is a test question?' asked Powell.

'It is my question,' replied the alderman testily.

'What I should do or not do does not affect my attitude to war in general: that is the general slaughter of each other by millions of men – the deliberate slaughter in cold blood as a means of settling international dispute.'

Mayor Greenland ('Are you prepared to stand by your country?') and Alderman James ('Would you allow a German to bayonet your mother without resisting?') spoke over each other.

'I refuse to take part in any machinery of war,' returned Powell, telling the alderman: 'I should defend her, but I should not think it necessary to take life to do it.'

'Have you a conscientious objection to fighting?' asked Alderman Watts.

'Yes, the deepest objection I have,' replied Powell.

After it transpired that Powell had refused a recommendation that he enlist with the RAMC – 'that would be relieving someone else to do what I object to do,' he declared – the tribunal issued a certificate of exemption from combatant services, but refused to grant an absolute exemption. Powell asked the chairman for an explanation.

'I shall give you no reason,' snapped the mayor.

The tribunal did grant absolute exemption later to Ernest J. Wilson, a foreman at S. Wright's Herefordshire Fruit Company. (The following year Wright revealed himself to be a pacifist.) Wilson had told the tribunal: 'To me all war is wrong and I cannot have anything to do with it.'

Stanley Powell had a lone supporter: Charles Dowers of 29 Newtown Road, who wrote to the *Hereford Times* complaining about the tribunal's refusal to provide reasons for their decision. Powell returned to the tribunal, this time under Chairman Sir John Cotterell, to appeal for total exemption. He and Cotterell clashed repeatedly throughout the hearing, which was adjourned for a week. When it reconvened that April Powell again went head to head with Cotterell: 'I don't come here pleading for anything. I demand my legal rights under the Act,' Powell told him.

'We don't want a speech,' retorted Sir John, dismissing the appeal. Sir John and his fellow tribunal members were accurately reflecting the strength of public feeling against men with a conscientious objection to joining the fight. Public indignation against Powell and others was growing. One Leominster resident warned that these 'shirkers should clear out and seek refuge in Germany or Turkey or else be put to work to look after lunatics'. An alternative suggestion that conscientious objectors should be forced to form burial parties on the front was challenged by another newspaper reader: 'Men who have fallen, doing their duty, are to be laid in their last resting place by cowards who shelter behind their "consciences" to get out of their part in this great struggle for home and civilisation?'

Other letter writers agreed: 'If a man will not serve his country he should not enjoy her laws for protection,' declared one as the bishop weighed in with his own views. 'To refuse to take part in [war] work is to stand apart in selfish isolation repudiating the claims of humanity and our obligation to the state for the advantages it brings to us and the protection of the law.' He urged conscientious objectors to undertake non-combatant duties as did doctors, nurses, Quakers, the YMCA and the Red Cross.

At the height of the controversy William Anderton and 19-year-old Henry Watkins Cooper, both of 19 Drapers Lane, Leominster, and Arthur Alexander Clery, an electrical engineer from 94 South Street, appeared before Leominster Town Tribunal as conscientious objectors. Absolute exemption would be refused to all three. Like Stanley Powell, William Anderton was initially granted exemption from combatant services on condition that he join the RAMC. While Powell had refused the option, Anderton agreed. The Medical Corps, however, were to turn him down.

Arthur Clery was given a dressing down by Tribunal Chairman, Mayor H. Goding. 'You are content to hold a good position while others shed their blood for you. [You] are having a very comfortable time of it. Think of those who are fighting.' Clery was to join the Quaker Friends Ambulance Unit working at Birmingham and York hospitals and aiding the wounded on board the ferries that carried them back from France. He would be awarded a Red Cross medal for his services. Aubrey Ross of 12 Bridge Street was, as a member of the evangelical Leominster Open Brethren, another objector. He would serve with the RAMC as a stretcher bearer in France. Back in Hereford, Plymouth Brethren Leonard Stewart Cox, a clerk at Edwards, Russell and Baldwin living in Lingen Avenue, Hereford, and Ambrose Yates, a railway signalman from St Owen Gate, both appealed for exemption on the grounds of their consciences. Cox was turned down, Yates' case adjourned, while in Ledbury two teachers, 23-year-old R.H. Wyatt and 34-year-old Harold Mostyn Watkins from Colwall's Downs School, also requested exemption.

'Would you object to making munitions?' asked the Ledbury chairman, Spencer Brickham.

'I wish to have nothing to do with warfare in any respect,' replied Wyatt. Both men were refused as were an Aston Ingham fruit farmer and a 19-year-old Gorsley builder (neither named by the press) when they appeared before the Ross Tribunal at the Union Offices Board Room. The builder was Evan J.S. Watkins of Yew Tree Cottage, Gorsley. Chairman Mr T. Preece could not contain his anger and told one: 'Go home man and consult your conscience again – we consider conscientious objection an absolute unworthy one on the part of any Englishman.' If such remarks echoed popular sentiment, they alarmed those who believed that the right not to fight was one of the liberties being fought for.

By the middle of the year, fears were growing that the war would be lost and Britain invaded by Germany. It persuaded the Hereford Tribunal to insist that membership of the Volunteer Training Corps (VTC) should be made a condition of exemption: the VTC undertook guard duties and relieved Regular and Territorial men then on defence duties to join the front line. Anyone who refused to become a member of the VTC could expect a rough ride from the tribunals.

In July Edmund Jones, who was seeking exemption on grounds of conscience along with Edmund Greg Wilson, suffered an acrimonious confrontation with Hereford City Tribunal Chairman Frank James. Wilson, who was prepared to take a non-combatant role, was allowed to have his case heard in private. But Edmund Jones's case was heard in public. He produced letters from Mr E.J. Peters from the Eignbrook Adult School and Revd Herbert Davies from the Cloisters confirming that he had long held his pacifist views. They incurred the wrath of the chairman.

'You ask me to believe that you can sit here and say your conscience allows you to live in a home in Hereford in comfort, and work and eat your food, none of which you could get but from the British Navy. You dare to tell me that is your conscience?'

'I am stating my opinion,' replied Jones.

'My opinion is that you should be thoroughly ashamed of yourself,' roared James at which point there were cries of 'Shame!' directed at the chairman from friends of Jones who had come to the session to support him. Momentarily taken aback, the chairman threatened to clear the court, telling Jones: 'You stay at home and take the benefit of what our soldiers and sailors are doing.' Nevertheless the tribunal, unusually, granted Jones exemption. Were they swayed by Jones's supporters? Bricklayer and mason Henry J. Cole, who preached at Kingsthorne Ebenezer Gospel Hall, also came before Hereford Rural Tribunal for refusing to do any work on the Sabbath. He was exempted for a month in order to be allowed to join the Ambulance Brigade or Red Cross, but not before Chairman Mr Swabey castigated him for eating a good dinner cooked by his wife every Sunday. 'You do not object to other people doing work for you?'

The tribunal decisions which appeared to favour conscientious objectors exasperated a letter writer from Much Birch, who wondered how such people dared call themselves Britishers. But the tribunal chairman, Frank James, had overstepped the mark. In another letter to the *Hereford Times* Revd Davies reminded readers that the tribunals' duty was only 'to ascertain whether or not the individual before them did really hold such "scruples" and whether those scruples were genuine.' The government required that 'men who apply on conscience grounds should be able to feel that they are being judged by a tribunal that will deal fairly with their case'.

'Granted that a man may hold sincerely that it is against Christian ethics to take any part in military service, it requires today far more moral courage to be true to that faith than to go along with the crowd. To taunt such men with cowardice (of all things) is surely quite beside the mark,' wrote Davies. He added that, personally, he did not see why anyone would refuse to assist the wounded, but his appeal to common sense did not sit comfortably with many people. In the same issue of that week's newspaper the deaths were announced of Major Graham Bosanquet, son of Admiral Sir Day Hort Bosanquet of Brom-y-close, Llanwarne; Capt Francis Burrough, the fifth son of the late Revd C. Burrough of Eaton Bishop; 2nd Lt Eric William Manning Price, the grandson of the Marden rector Revd David Price (the village's previous rector, Revd D. Ellis Rowlands, was now serving as an army chaplain); and Lt Leslie Day, eldest son of Mr and Mrs T. Day of Prospect House, Ross.

Nevertheless the Revd Lang preached a sermon in Leominster in support of William Anderton, who, as related above, had been refused absolute exemption by the town's tribunal. In his address Lang protested: 'It is easy to talk loudly and to use such expressions as "beastly, brutal Germans" and "butchering little children", but the tribunal[s] are not there to hector and bully but to find out if these men really hold the views they profess. It is a sad day when men who have responded to the call of Christ are so assailed, tormented, insulted and treated in the fashion that William Anderton has been.' Making no friends amongst his congregation, he insisted: 'This war, which was to maintain liberty, has destroyed liberty.'

Anderton was court-martialled for disobeying orders in the non-combatant corps and sentenced to two years' hard labour. Sent to Wormwood Scrubs Prison he was eventually classified as a Class A Objector by the Central Tribunal and sent to mend roads in Suffolk. He finished the war in Dartmoor Prison. In May it was reported that Stanley Powell had been brought before a court martial in North Wales and sentenced to two years' hard labour for refusing to obey military orders.

Teacher Harold Watkins, who had been refused exemption, was arrested under DORA and brought to court that June. The magistrates' clerk explained that since Watkins had been registered under the National Registration Act, but had not attested, he was deemed to have enlisted on March 2. He had technically disobeyed orders to report to Ledbury Drill Hall on May 10 and was arrested.

'I know that legally I am a soldier, but morally I am not,' Harold Watkins told the court, adding: 'I know there is a Defence of the Realm Act, and I feel that there is a defence of the realm's conscience.' He was fined 2 shillings and ordered to be taken by a recruiting officer to Shrewsbury. As he left court he turned to the press bench. 'Please report that I have been treated with kindness and consideration by the police,' he told reporters. In July Watkins would be sentenced to 84 days' hard labour for refusing to put on a khaki uniform. He would be court-martialled five times and spend time in prison at Shrewsbury, Wormwood Scrubs, Winchester, Winson Green in Birmingham, Strangeways in Manchester, Wakefield and Northallerton. The Gorsley builder Evan Watkins was similarly taken to Copthorne Barracks for forcible enlistment, court-martialled and sentenced to two years' hard labour. By August, having been transferred to Wormwood Scrubs prison, Watkins, like many other conscientious objectors, appeared before a Central Tribunal, found 'genuine' and allowed to join a Home Office scheme mending roads at Clare in Suffolk. The following August he was sent to work at Wood Farm, Sunk Island near Hull.

Leominster's Henry Watkins Cooper would spend time in prison at Winson Green in Birmingham and Wormwood Scrubs before ending up at the Dyce Stone quarry in Aberdeenshire where many conscientious objectors were put to work.

Some weeks before Watkins first appeared at the Hereford Tribunal, city builder William Bolt had attended to appeal on behalf of his horseman, Harold Farr. Bolt had contracts with His Majesty's Office of Works and was struggling to manage the business with only over-aged labour on hand. The tribunal granted temporary exemption to August 1 on hearing that Bolt's son Bertram had been killed only the week before.

Bertam Bolt's story was all too common: in April he had given notice at Messrs Evans where he was deputy manager and enlisted as a private with the KSLI. He took the train to Shrewsbury barracks and on 15 April returned to the family home, Hawthorns at 88 Baysham Street, on 48-hours' leave. He dispatched some of his new visiting cards ('2nd LIEUT B.L. BOLT 6th BATTALION, KSLI') and noted on a fresh page of his diary: 'Sunday April 16. Wet. Eignbrook in morning. Short walk with E in afternoon. Left Hereford by 8 o/c train.' That evening he was in camp at Prees Heath preparing with his pals 'Dallow, Jinks and Capt Spenser' to catch the morning train to London. By Tuesday morning they were boarding the Folkestone ferry for Boulogne and four days after bidding 'E' goodbye, Bertram Bolt was on the front line: 'Thursday April 27. Lovely day. Aeroplanes busy. Impossible to get a wink of sleep all day or night. We were heavily strafed about mid-day with a bit of every-thing pretty well. 3 casualties in my Company.' The last entry in Bolt's diary was May 10. He was killed on the road to Armentières after spending only 29 days as a soldier.

2nd Lieutenant Bertram Bolt lasted just 28 days as a soldier on the front line in France. One of four sons, Bertram of Baysham Street, Hereford kept a diary of his days at war. The final entry reads: 'Nothing very exciting happened'. A temporary cross was erected over his grave at Armentières: 'Died of wounds 13 May 1916'. (Photo: Michael Bolt)

His father William called at the offices of the *Hereford Times* in Maylord Street to help compile the memorial notice: 'We regret to announce the death in France of Lieutenant B.L. Bolt, 23, of the KSLI. His eldest brother, Pte Harold Bolt, is a motor driver in Egypt and Pte Percival is in Naval Air Service.' The newspaper, under editor Charles Bex, was striving to cover the news in difficult circumstances. With two of its five reporters in the forces, the editor asked for 11 employees, from monotype operator Charles Jones to reporters Albert John Garstone and Percy Harry Hitchman, to be exempt.

The newspaper did manage to find the manpower to report on a memorial service in the city that summer for the Secretary of State for War, Lord Kitchener. Kitchener had drowned when his ship, *HMS Hampshire*, with Hereford seaman Dick Simpson amongst the 644 sailors on board, put to sea in a gale. Bad weather had kept the mine sweepers in dock. *Hampshire* ran into a mine and sank off the Orkney Islands. Dick Simpson was one of only 12 survivors. 'I am all safe. Don't worry,' he telegrammed his mother.

It was against this gloomy background that the county was struck by a domestic tragedy: seven children taking part in a benefit concert for the KSLI at the Garrick Theatre

The talented Breinton artist Brian Hatton enlisted in the cavalry, the Worcestershire Yeomanry. He would be killed in action in the Sinai Desert on Easter Sunday morning, 23 April 1916. His family played an active part on the home front, accommodating Belgian refugees at the family home, Mount Craig in Broomy Hill, while his younger sisters, Ailsa and Marjorie, volunteered for farm work.
(Photo: Herefordshire Museum Service)

died in a fire. The deaths of 45-year-old Lt-Col Edward Luard, husband of Louise of South Bank, at Flanders and the artist Brian Hatton, killed in action in the Sinai Desert on Easter Sunday morning (at Hatton's memorial service Holmer's Revd Francis Tuke referred to the artist as that 'modest genius'), barely earned a mention in the press as newspapermen reflected on the deaths of 5-year-old Connie Bragg, 6-year-old Winnie Mailes, 7-year-old Violet Corey, 10-year-old Phyllis White, 12-year-old Cissie Beavan and 13-year-old Nellie Rutherford. Later, 5-year-old Peggy Baird would die of her injuries.

The benefit concert had been organised by Winnie's mother, Mrs Mailes of Ivy House, Bewell Street, to boost the comfort funds of the Hereford Territorials and Shropshire Regulars. During a snow dance scene, which involved 40 children being pelted with snowballs of cotton wool, a child's dress had suddenly caught fire. Panicking, she rushed about the stage now scattered with burning cotton wool balls. In front of a horrified audience the fire spread from child to child as parents and friends scrambled on stage to try and smother the flames. The source of the fire at the theatre, which had been rebuilt with modern fire safety features

16 months earlier, remained a mystery. The only clue came from one seriously injured girl, 10-year-old Linda Illman of 3 Henrietta Place, Park Street. She told her mother, Eleanor: 'It was a man with a match.' Some days later on a cold and blustery morning khaki-clad soldiers bore five of the little coffins through the streets to the cathedral. The bell ringers tolled on a muffled peal while the city shops closed and house windows were shuttered as a mark of respect. Theatre patrons were offered reduced-price tickets

As a child Brian Hatton had been fascinated by horses. Before the war he drew and painted the animals at Warham Court where farmer James Powell bred shire horses. When war came Brian enlisted in a cavalry regiment, the Worcestershire Yeomanry, and continued sketching and drawing until he was killed in action in the Sinai Desert on Easter Sunday in 1916.

Above, An Advance Guard Patrolling a Road;

Left, Enemy In Sight;

Opposite, the bleakly titled Civilisation.

(Images: Herefordshire Museum Service)

to performances and asked to donate the difference to a fund for the children. The fund raised £500 and a memorial child's cot was placed in the children's ward of the General Hospital in memory of the dead girls.

Little Linda Illman's father was serving in Gallipoli and first-hand accounts of those terrible days in the Dardanelles continued to reach home. One tragedy involved 51-year-old colour sergeant Bill Faulkner, a well-known Hereford man on service with

Right: George Denis Davies, left, aged 24; David Charles Ivor Davies, aged 20, and James Edgar Davies aged 13 and then in the Officers Training Corps, pictured in October 1914.

Below: The Davies family before the war outside the family home in Cornewall Street, Hereford. Left to right, back row: Llewellyn, parents Elizabeth and Richard, Gwen; middle row: baby Glyn with George and Ivor, front: May and Edgar. George was invalided out of the army in 1917 after being sent to serve in Egypt, having contracted rheumatic fever and suffering frostbite at Gallipoli. He wrote a postcard home: 'Keep smiling. Am quite safe.' (Photos: Pat and Don Davies)

his son, Sgt C.F. Faulkner. He wrote to his mother, breaking the news of Bill Faulkner's death: 'I hardly know where to start this letter. I am so very upset. We landed at 6am, and came under shelling. The first to be hit in our regiment was Stanley Mailes.' (He was the son of the butcher at Hereford Butter Market.) 'But after a little while the shelling died down and we had dinner. Then towards evening we were ordered to go into the firing line. I should think we had gone two miles when the enemy started to shell us. Well, mum I can hardly steady myself to tell you that one of the bullets from the shells hit dad. [At first] I could not find dad anywhere. It was getting dark so I made off in the direction of the beach. However when I got up next morning I was told that he had been picked up, and was taken to the hospital, but was quite dead, so I never saw him again.'

More than 50 of the King Street Adult School's former pupils had served at Gallipoli after joining the Herefordshire Regiment. Three of them, stretcher bearer Wood, Drummer Davies and Pte W.A. Hicks, returned to the school to relate their experiences. Pte Wood spoke graphically of men 'falling like rabbits after landing at Suvla Bay' while Davies explained how, having been wounded during the shelling of the beach at Salt Lake, which he likened to the Lugg Meadows, he still managed to return alive. Hicks recalled the great storm that left them wading in waist-deep water. Some, he said, had been simply swept away.

Wives and mothers waited anxiously for news, knowing that so many of their men were involved in the conflict, but front line soldiers were as reluctant to elaborate on their experiences as they would be in their later years. George Davies who had been badly wounded at Gallipoli returned to his old church, the Hereford Baptist Church in Commercial Street, to try and explain how soldiers felt about their loved ones while fighting on the front line. He recalled how, on the second day of the landings at Suvla Bay, he had written a postcard home: 'Keep smiling. Am quite safe. Everything lovely.' Now invalided out of the army, George, the son of Prudential insurance manager Richard Davies of 4 Cornewall Street, told his fellow Baptists: 'I well remember writing this postcard in ghastly company, my lips cracking for a drink of water and my younger brother and some pals missing. The chief concern is to stop our people worrying about us back home,' he told his listeners. 'It's no use worrying over the boys out yonder: it only upsets them and you. Just pray for them hourly.'

Letters from the front continued to arrive. The vicar of Lyde, Revd G. Bosanquet, allowed his nephew Gerard Ganley's letters to be published after the young man was taken prisoner of war. His ship, *HMS Arabis*, had been sunk in the North Sea in February. 'When the torpedo hit us the ship lurched to go down [and] everyone made a jump for it. Rescued by a German destroyer with the captain and the ship's doctor, I was given a hot drink and put to bed.' He added, perhaps to pacify the censor amongst his captors: 'I must say that the German officers treated us very well.'

Another letter arrived at 5 Highmore Street, Westfields addressed to Mr and Mrs Jones, the parents of Charles Jones, a signaller aboard *HMS Broke*. *Broke* was involved in the Battle of Jutland and Jones was full of praise for his commander, Walter Lingen Allen whose parents, Mr and Mrs Allen, lived at Southbank House. A newspaper man sent round to interview Jones when he arrived home on leave described how *HMS Broke*, having given chase to a German cruiser which they had torpedoed, came under attack from other German ships. 'It soon put us out of action. Our vessel was riddled from stem to stern like a lid of a pepper box,' reported Jones. *Broke* lost 48 men killed with 10 missing and 40 wounded.

The armoured cruiser *HMS Warrior* foundered in the battle and Seaman Blake from The Nursery, Ross, who was serving on board wrote home: 'The English people have every reason to be proud of the Navy.'

Heroic stories from soldiers and sailors like Davies, Ganley, Jones and Blake persuaded many local men to enlist. One was even driven to suicide when the army turned him down because of his poor eyesight: former Hereford railwayman Charles Jones drank poison after being refused by the army for the third time. The local tribunals, meanwhile, had served their purpose of sending many of the more reluctant men away to war.

The absence of so many men on the home front compelled the Board of Agriculture to turn to the women and in May HWAC called a public meeting at Hereford's Assembly Hall to allow a Miss Day from the Board of Trade and Mr Allsebrook from the Board of Agriculture to reveal plans for employing more women on farms. In the light of government proposals to introduce enforced tillage, an appeal was about to be launched for a land army of 400,000 women designed to relieve the pressure on farmers.

Traditional resistance to women farmworkers was still strong; even the meeting's chairman, Mr Turner, offered the less than helpful comment that 'contrary to a present belief' women could be 'most useful in the lighter jobs'. Allsebrook, however, commended Docklow farmer Lawson Miller who, he said, was full of admiration for his two new women workers, one a former milliner the other a dressmaker. He told the largely male audience: 'the hand that rocks the baby rules the waves: well, the hand that hoes the

'It's a mistake to think that women can do anything on the farm,' declared one Hereford official. Yet many county women volunteered for the new Women's Land Army and proved themselves more than capable. This group posed for the photographer at Withington with their male foreman. (Photo: Herefordshire Museums)

A Land Army girl posing for a studio photo with what the photographer and she presumably thought was a suitably rustic backdrop.
(Photo: Herefordshire Libraries)

turnips also rules the waves'. Miss Day warned that the day was drawing closer when the country would be put on rations. (After the failure of voluntary rationing in 1917 compulsory rationing would be introduced in early 1918.) It was the duty of town as well as country women to ask: 'Am I doing the work most needed by my country?'

As the Farmers' Aid Women's Society called for a parish-by-parish list of farmers willing to employ women, plans were announced for crèches to be provided in Hereford to allow local mothers to work in the fields. Yet there remained considerable antipathy towards the idea of women coping with the demands of farmwork. When Percy Jones of Redbrook Farm, Bullingham appeared before the Hereford Tribunal, the military representative, Capt Morgan, suggested that women might assist on his farm. 'Oh, women won't work,' asserted a fellow tribunal member. His views were echoed by another on the panel: 'It's a mistake to think that women can do anything on the farm.' The issue of female labour rose again when John Bolt of Breinton appealed on behalf of his son who did the milking. The son was exempted until May 1, but one tribunal member asked Bolt: 'Cannot women do milking?'

'You can't get 'em,' replied Bolt adding that he had no place to lodge a woman. Another member agreed. It was unreasonable, he explained, to expect a woman to go milking from Hereford at four in the morning. ('Take a taxi,' muttered one disgruntled tribunal member, Mr Andrews.)

The better-off women and mothers who employed domestic servants continued to keep themselves busy with charity work. The Soldiers and Sailors' Restroom at Barrs Court station would benefit from Christmas gifts of bundles of holly from farmer's wife Mrs Bellamy at Penallt (her son Arthur was still serving abroad with the RAMC), cakes and mistletoe from Miss Joyce Wear and a ham from the City Arms Hotel. In the run-up to Christmas the restroom would cater for almost 700 men and prompt a grateful Pte A. Lewis to write of 'such kindness you can never forget'. Nurses at the voluntary hospitals were also grateful for gifts. Miss Bulmer supported Walney House, Dorothy Dymond supported her former home, now a Red Cross hospital, Hampton Grange, and Mrs Hawkins of Thinghill supported Beechwood. Sarnesfield Hospital was provided with a Christmas goose by Mrs Lane of The Mere and a brace of rabbits to go with the bird by Staunton on Wye parish.

Hereford's Dean Leigh was by now spearheading a campaign to raise funds for a Hereford Diocese rest hut for fighting troops (£25 was soon raised) while the newly widowed Louise Luard of South Bank continued her efforts to support the ten local KSLI men held prisoners of war. Each man was adopted by a lady who oversaw the dispatch of parcels of food, warm underclothes and bread (on which Mrs Luard had spent almost £20). Lady Helen Lucas-Tooth provided funds for a new substantially built and well-appointed parish hall at Holme Lacy. It was opened in memory of her two sons, Robert and Douglas, who had been killed in the war. Mrs Foster from Brockhampton donated funds for x-ray apparatus at Ross Hospital.

Charitable donations did not come solely from the wealthy. As the Mynde estate was broken up and sold following the death of Sir James Rankin, an appeal was raised to help war veteran and amputee William Powell to buy his own place, Sams Pool, near Little Hill. A miner from Abertillery sent £1 to the fund.

Five of the Powell brothers who lived at The Stars, Orcop went to war. (From the left, back row: Reg, Fred, George, William, Bert, Ted and Leonard; in front Mr and Mrs Powell and daughter Eddie). All returned safe except William, who lost his leg. A public campaign raised funds which allowed William to buy the nearby smallholding Sams Pool, part of the Rankin estate. William went on to run the Spread Eagle at Walford. (Photo: Angus Brymer)

Working women struggled to manage. A 25-year-old music teacher, Dorothy Craick from Wyeside, Hoarwithy, ended up in court after she pocketed the money she had collected for the Serbian Relief Fund from the likes of Mrs Lily Wyndham Smith of Aramstone Court, the Hentland vicar Revd D.R. Evans and Pencoyd schoolmaster Albert Coombes. She was discharged on a technicality, not detailed in the newspaper report, prompting Justice Avory to observe: 'You have had a very narrow escape.' Craick was not the only educationalist to appear before magistrates. Francis James Smith's efforts to join the ranks of the county's school inspectors were thwarted when a suspicious clerk re-examined Smith's birth certificate. Smith of Holmer Road turned out to be a Mr Wilson who had stolen the certificate and passed himself off as being above military age. The fact that he had abandoned a wife and nine children in Oxford did not impress Hereford magistrates, who sentenced him to five months' imprisonment.

Sometime later a Mrs Perry from Little Doward, Symonds Yat was brought before Harewood End police court for stealing 3s 6d worth of clothing from a washing line at The Pound, Whitchurch. Her soldier husband, home on leave from the RAMC, was distressed to learn that this was her second offence, the first having been committed while he was away at war. He pleaded with magistrates not to impose a prison sentence for the sake of their four children. The magistrates obliged with a 15 shillings fine and a stern warning.

Fines were also handed down to a Miss Elliott from the Withington Dairy in Broad Street on the technical charge of providing watered-down milk. The watering down had been carried out by delivery man Albert Johnson of 2 Wye Street: he was fined 40 shillings (£2) and Miss Elliott 10 shillings. Meanwhile a 15-year-old girl, Lucy Preece of Whitecross Road, was sent to reformatory school for three years for pickpocketing three purses from patrons at the Garrick Theatre. She appeared in court alongside Jack and James Richardson, who were sentenced to six strokes of the birch each for maliciously damaging an apple tree in Mr C.F. Beakbane's Aylestone Hill orchard. 'I hope they give 'em heavy,' the father told the magistrate.

Other women who fell foul of the law included Jane Burton, accused of aiding her husband, Welsh Regiment deserter Reginald James Lovell, to hide from the authorities. The police told Hereford magistrates that they had raided a gypsy camp to round up men of military age who had been deemed to have enlisted, but had not done so. Gypsies David John (29), Henry John (24), Nelson (24) and William Vaughan (34) were arrested while Lovell was discovered hiding under a pile of straw on which his wife, Jane, was seated. She strenuously denied being his wife, but was fined 20 shillings (£1).

More distressing was the case of a married woman, Gertie Owens from Abergavenny, who had been lodging with a widow, Maria Watkins in Stanhope Street, Hereford. She had given birth, in secret, to a stillborn child. When arrested and charged with the concealment of the birth by PC Spendlove, the frightened young woman told the policeman: 'It was stillborn. I did nothing to it. I could tell you the man?' The charge was dismissed.

The soldiers caused their own share of problems. In September passers-by in Barrs Court Road had been alarmed to see a uniformed man throw himself from a passing train and run away towards Aylestone Hill. It was Pte William Dixon of the King's Liverpool Regiment who had escaped custody on his way to 12 months' imprisonment at Hereford Detention Barracks. He was arrested later at Old Eign Hill.

Soldiers' families, meanwhile, often found it difficult to make ends meet. When a Ross soldier's wife and mother of five children was hospitalised, the town Guardians took in her children. She was receiving 27 shillings (12 shillings for herself and 15 shillings for her children), yet the Guardians charged her £1 a week instead of the 15 shillings allocated for the children. The wife of another private complained: 'I have to keep myself and five children on 14 shillings and 6 pence a week. As I am only a private's wife, my allowances are 5 shillings for the first child, 3 shillings and 6 pence for the next and 2 shillings each for the other three children, which works out at 2 shillings 11 pence a week each and it will take some scheming to keep them properly clothed and fed. As I am very delicate I cannot help the home with any earnings.'

By mid-winter, however, there was a new source of income for those with a stronger constitution: the munitions. Twelve months earlier the *Hereford Times* had reported on 'the probability of a munitions factory being established at Hereford. The office of the Government Munition[s] Department are in correspondence with the officers of the Hereford Corporation with this object in view, and the matter is now under consideration. We hear on good authority that Herefordshire is the only county in England without a building solely used for the manufacture of munitions of war. If Hereford complies with the suggestion … it would lead to the employment of a large number of hands, men and women.'

The fiery Welsh reformer David Lloyd George, Minister of Munitions since 1915, was behind the plan. Lloyd George had turned the bumbling, male-dominated armaments industry into a relatively streamlined, government-owned manufacturer powered by women. In doing so he achieved more for women's suffrage than the suffragettes themselves. Having defeated Clydeside's ship workers over their opposition to 'dilution' (using unskilled or semi-skilled workers, mostly women, to do jobs normally done by union members), the minister commissioned the expansion of Woolwich Arsenal and ordered a series of shell, projectile (for heavier munitions) and explosives filling factories to be built around the country. Local management boards were tasked with overseeing the construction and the running of the plants.

Rotherwas to the south of the city was earmarked as a filling factory. For security reasons the local press did not cover the construction of the factory although in July they reported that the August public holidays had been cancelled 'by the Ministry of Munitions'. Later Mayor Greenland expressed his concern over the number of workers that were 'expected to arrive shortly' and how they might be housed: the council was then considering a £70,000 housing scheme to provide accommodation with rents set at 11 shillings a week.

The Munitions department was exempt from many local government statutes and when it ordered the construction of latrines at Hereford Market (they were to serve the Rotherwas construction workers, housed in the market sheds) Alderman E.L. Wallis complained publicly about the Ministry's cavalier attitude. (The Wallis family were soon preoccupied with more pressing matters: in October, one of their sons returned home wounded.)

Events involving the influx of workers to Rotherwas soon began to impact on the city. In October seven building workers were charged with a variety of minor offences after a police raid on their sleeping quarters. In November police were called to intervene in a fight between foreman Robert Wade from Horsham and Charles Piper who, claimed Wade, had made disparaging comments about his landlady. That same month a journeyman carpenter from Portishead, Henry Harris, was run over and killed by a light engine driven by Mark Proctor at the factory site, and later that year the local newspapers flagged up a case at the King's Bench against Messrs John Mowlem and Co over 'a munition factory, although unfinished [and] involving the sum of £200,000'. Rotherwas couldn't be named for reasons of national security.

One 11-year-old schoolboy, Alfred Evans, looked on as the factory rose above the river meadows. He was helping out at the Wye Hotel nearby, run by his grandparents. 'There had been a hundred acres of some of the finest wheat in the country standing there in August: they cleared that and built the factory. It was in operation in a very short time and it employed thousands.' Since many of the munition workers were expected to come from the city a temporary footbridge was attached to the side of the railway bridge over the river near Hampton Park hill. 'Then they put a path all the way across the field that we called the Croft,' Alf recalled.

As the building continued, Alf carried on with his education. Although his family were Protestants, Alf attended the local Catholic school run by mostly Irish nuns at Lower Bullingham. These were turbulent times in Irish affairs and the little Bullingham school did not escape their effects. Aside from the Easter Uprising in Dublin, Irish rebels had reportedly assassinated a local squire and his wife from nearby Dinedor. 'Captain Price from Dinedor Court, who had property in Ireland, went over there and while he and his wife were out riding he was taken from his horse and shot,' Alf remembered. 'When our priest, Father Morrison, came along to school afterwards he started going on about Black and Tans and convicts being let out of Dartmoor.' The patriotic young Protestant scrambled to his feet: 'I called him a liar and walked out.' Five days later his mother received a note from the Mother Superior, Sister Arundel, instructing him to return. Alf went back to school expecting to be caned for his troubles. His protest, however, had been noted: 'Sister told me off, but the Protestants that were upset didn't have any more Roman Catholic teaching and Father Morrison left shortly after.'

By now the fortunes of the Wye Hotel had improved considerably with the influx of building workers. 'Since we came under the Defence of the Realm Act we were only allowed to open for one hour. The navvies' tea boys used to come up at 11 o'clock, pay over the money and we'd hand the beer over. You couldn't use the beer engines because of the froth so we put the beer in galvanised baths, and you'd be dipping the mugs in the baths and putting it out like that. The place would be packed for one hour.'

Back in the city meanwhile, Chief Constable Frank Richardson had complained about the number of drunken soldiers in the streets and of women spending their army money on drink. He had told the city magistrates sitting at one of the 1916 brewster sessions that 'there is as much drinking going on now as in normal times' and he called for the 18 pubs that lined Widemarsh Street to be reduced by half. He had, however, a worthy opponent in the brewery's representative, Mr Wadsworth, who pointed out that the number of convictions for drunkenness had actually fallen between 1914 (149) and 1916 (86). After Wadsworth's intercession the Chief Constable's objections to relicensing the Elephant and Castle in St Peters Street, the Oxford Arms in Widemarsh Street and the corporation-owned Number 10, also in Widemarsh Street but on the corner with Maylord Street, were overruled.

Yet the Medical Officer for Health, Dr J.W. Miller, had also warned of a rise in the number of deaths due to the abuse of alcohol by 'persons of all classes' in his annual report. (The fact was noted by the Bishop of Hereford, a leading campaigner for the state control of all alcohol sales.) Miller outlined the chief causes of death, excluding those from armaments: heart disease, cancer, old age and pneumonia. However, although he noted a worrying dip in the birth rate, with 428 births in the city during 1915, he reported that people's general health had, in spite of these austere times, improved. Miller attributed the improvement to better housing, a corporation house-building programme having recently rehoused 62 families from a former city slum. (He added that there were still areas for improvement, singling out the city's 12 dairies and 22 milking cowsheds: 'Often no attempt is made to remove dirt from udders and flanks of the cows, with the result that some of this dirt finds its way into the milk.')

In November Alderman Greenland, who was handing over the mayoral reins to Councillor Edmund Dymond, had sent door-to-door canvassers out in search of accommodation for the munitions workers who, towards the end of the year, began to sign up at the Hereford Labour Exchange. After several hundred were said to have attended a service organised by local Baptists at the Kemble Theatre, the *Hereford Times* mused over how they were to be entertained out of work. 'It is most desirable that the movement should be started as soon as possible rather than wait till the munitions workers have arrived.'

The YMCA, which was already hosting entertainments for the construction workers, was expected to help, as was the Kemble Theatre which had recently featured 'excellent turns' by Elsie Bowers at the piano and the Lever Bros comedians. The Garrick, in competition, was screening *Still Waters Run Deep* starring Lady Tree. Other suggestions for amusing 'the thousands of women workers who are to be added to our population' as the *Hereford Times* put it, ranged from gardening clubs ('over 500 gardeners had taken advantage of such a scheme in Birmingham') to river swimming. Even before the munitioneers arrived there was little to be done on a Sunday except go fishing (the Wye Board of Conservators had failed earlier that May to prevent Sunday fishing) or work in the garden: George Lovelock from St James wrote to the newspapers encouraging people to plant more of 'this profitable and useful article of food', the potato.

Some, however, were less worried about the housing or entertainment issues and more concerned with the moral well-being of the munitioneers. Mrs Greenland convened a meeting at the Town Hall to discuss the formation of women's patrols. The patrols, it was decided, would not be tasked with 'rescuing' workers but 'as befriending the girls in their own interests'. Nevertheless Mrs Dymond, Mrs Luard, the dean and Mr Phillips from the National Union of Women Workers expected the women's patrols to put a check on any 'unseemly behaviour'. That possibility had increased with the introduction of a citywide night-time blackout following concerns over the possibility of zeppelin attacks. Earlier in the year the manager of Pearl Assurance in St Peters Square, Thomas Howell, was fined £1 for neglecting the blackout while chorister George Holloway was said to be 'temporarily stunned' when, after leaving choral society rehearsals, he strode into a pillar box in the darkened street.

As the builders departed, the first factory recruits assembled in a hall at the factory to hear the standard lecture delivered to new girls by the superintendent. 'The building of National Filling Factory No. 14 was started on July 11. It contains over 25 miles of railway, ten miles of footway, three miles of special, explosive-proof mastic road, and our farm which supplies daily milk free to those in filling,' they were told.

'Our first munitions were delivered safely on 20 November. We expect to quadruple production by February and again by May. And we are proud to be on the way to becoming the sixth biggest National Filling Factory in the nation.'

The supervisor made light of any possible dangers: 'I may remind you that you are working with explosives. They are no more dangerous than taking a train journey. But if you do something silly, there are serious consequences. It is for this reason the Factory is divided in two: the Dirty and Clean Ways. In Dirty Way there is no explosive. This, for example, is part of Dirty Way. In Clean Way there is explosive in store, in shell and in finished munitions. You will never, I repeat never, enter Clean Way without the necessary clothing and shoes or carrying any incendiary or sparking items. That includes cigarettes, confectionery (sugars can react with explosive), matches or any metal including button, hat pin, brooch or ring.'

Finally, after explaining that there was to be no paid leave for menstrual fatigue ('although your foreman will be sympathetic to your condition') she explained the purpose behind Filling Factory No. 14: 'We are making breech-loading shells for the Front Line Artillery. Ours and Chilwell are the only two in the nation so employed.

'You may think of the munition shell as a death-dealing instrument. It is not. The munition shell is a life saver. Thanks to the splendid co-operation of our artillery and our infantry in attack, and to the work of the male and female munitioneer, the munition shell is saving the lives of our boys on the Front Line. Remind yourself of that every day you are here.'

Our boys might have been relatively safe from our own munitions: German munitions, however, were killing and maiming the men of Herefordshire at an alarming rate. Former gamekeeper Pte W. Bryan of Old Lodge, Dorstone, was rendered disabled for the rest of his life after taking a shrapnel wound in France. L/Cpl Henry William Palin, the son of the former Linton vicar Revd Edward Palin, had been killed in action in France. So too was the eldest son of the late Count Lubienski, the former owner of the munitions factory site. Second Lt Henry E.C.H. Bodenham died in France, serving with the machine gun corps, known in the black-humoured parlance of the soldier as the suicide squad. (For one KSLI soldier, Pte J. Pritchard, number 431, the prospects of being sent to fight in France after Gallipoli proved too much: before the troops entrained, he cut his throat and died.)

With no sign of a resolution to the hostilities a letter writer to the Hereford papers reflected: 'War is no respecter of persons and not a few Herefordshire squires will never return to castle and court; and many Herefordshire homes are darkened. A local builder tells me ten of his men have been killed and no one writes to the papers to call attention to these dead heroes.'

Chapter 5

1917

1917 marked a significant turning point in the respective roles of working women and working horses, the former finding their feet, the latter looking increasingly redundant. Meanwhile the spectre of a food famine hung over Herefordshire.

February had seen Elsie Abel join the 800 women and 355 men now working at the new munitions factory. A Barry girl, she was the daughter of a Cardiff harbour dredger and his Liverpudlian wife. Elsie was also a valuable worker. On one occasion when fire broke out in her filling area she calmly plugged shells filled with explosives and closed all the windows to contain the fire. The Glasgow MP, William Anderson, told parliament she deserved a medal. Instead Elsie would end up in prison.

From the farmers' point of view 'the factory', as the Rotherwas munitions works was known, posed a serious threat to their labour force. Although the Labour Exchange had pledged not to take farm men for the factory, labourers were still leaving for the better wages on offer. One dairy farmer was said to have sold his herd after losing his dairymen to the munitions.

At their first meeting of the new year, the South Herefordshire farmers' leader A.J. Thompson observed that farmers were believed to be having the time of their lives. In reality, he said, feedstuffs and fertilisers were expensive and labour was desperately short. Farmers were receiving two-thirds of the pre-war price for their hay and straw yet paying record prices for supplies such as oil cake at £20 per ton. In addition the military was commandeering supplies: Mr Jones of Lower House, Kington had given up the last of his winter feed, a 12-ton hay rick, to the army and when the same fate befell Mr Hall at Ashton he lost three ewes as a consequence. 'A great many officers went about dictating to the farmers as if they were lords of creation,' complained Herefordshire War Agricultural Committee (HWAC)'s H.F. Russell.

Statistics for 1916 supported anecdotal evidence of hardship. The number of farms had fallen across the region (Herefordshire, Salop, Worcestershire, Gloucestershire, Wiltshire and Monmouthshire). Wheat production, still the county's biggest crop, had declined along with hops, down by 10%. Yet in May the government imported nearly 2,000 hundredweight of Californian hops, good shipping space which could have carried food, claimed Mr Thompson of the Hyde hop farm. More sheep, horses and cattle were being raised, but there were fewer pigs and, alarmingly, the amount of bare fallow land had increased by 9,000 acres. The county's farming was in crisis.

Based in East Street, HWAC represented the most powerful people in the farming community, men such as John Cotterell (of Garnons), Aldermen James Corner (who also chaired the Hereford Tribunal), H.F. Russell, A.P. Turner (of Fayre Oaks), E.C. Andrews (of Manor Farm), H.K. Foster, the Board of Agriculture's Mr Allsebrook, and Councillors (and farmers) Langford and Ballard from Colwall. The committee included Mr Duncan of Alexander and Duncan, Mr Smith (of Bidney) and the Farmers' Society's Mr Thompson, W.E. Taylor from Ross and J.P. Griffiths. Neither farm labourers nor women were represented on the committee. Farm workers' leader Sidney Box was bitter about their exclusion, pointing out that 1,600 members of the Labour Union were serving in the forces. Box also claimed that farmers were making 60% to 100% more on their produce than in peacetime so that, 'where a labourer was paid 15 shillings per week, £1 10 shillings is now due.' He added: 'And while they claim tenure for themselves, they deny the same right to the labourers.'

John Cotterell's recommendation that HWAC co-opt a farm worker was left on the table. Instead HWAC co-opted wealthy Tillington Court farmer Harold Barnett of Burghill Agricultural Society who offered the committee an interest-free £1,000 loan to buy ploughing tractors. The offer was shelved when the Board of Agriculture agreed to provide some machines.

The Board's new president, Rowland Prothero, met HWAC shortly after his appointment. Although he had family connections in the county (his mother, Emma, was from the Money-Kyrle family at Homme House, Much Marcle) his visit underlined Herefordshire's importance as a food producer. The president conceded that 'in Herefordshire they have "skinned" your farms of labour to a very great extent.' There were cheers of 'hear, hear' as he went on: 'Even if we do take more men from the country we are still firm in our resolution to increase the production of food.' Earlier in the year farmers were told that a third of the remaining eligible men in the county would be called up. It prompted 42-year-old Llewellyn Williams to walk into a barn and blow his brains out. His wife said at his inquest that, after he took on a larger farm at Norton Canon, the scarcity of labour had preyed on her husband's mind.

Prothero acknowledged that farmers had 'a great objection to half-time women' and assured the men that 'women labour for the future is not to be a substitution for the male labour'. But, he added, it was patriotic to employ them: 'Get the women on your register and get them to work whatever time they can give.'

Revealing plans for a new Women's Labour Department aimed at educated women, he warned that if the women were engaged on the farm they would expect to be billeted like ordinary soldiers, and paid the current wage. (The wage had risen to 25 shillings a week by mid-summer although at least one farmer was still advertising for a carter at 24 shillings a week 'with house and coal free and £5 harvest money – no cider, beer during harvest'.)

That March Prime Minister Lloyd George had warned: 'There are only a few weeks in which to sow the spring wheat, the oats, the barley and the potatoes. If you can use a spade or hoe, you MUST volunteer. Enrol today for National Service.' All men between

18 and 61 were urged to volunteer for farming, shipbuilding or woodland work and by May the first National Service Tribunals were being held in camera in Leominster, Ross and at Hereford Town Hall under sub-commissioner Maj H.P. Hamilton. (In July the tribunal at Ledbury, unhappy at the loss of yet more men, granted exemptions to all 31 cases brought before it after hearing that 350 trade assistants had been sent to the war from the urban district.)

Farmers, worried over having to pay the same wage to 'a poor substitute' as to a good man, received news of a fresh source of labour that spring. Seventy-five interned aliens were to be billeted at Ross Golf Club and made available to the farms at a mere 12/6d a week. The internees never arrived, although by June women were hoeing the corn on several farms, while Weobley District Council was paying local women workers 2s 6d a day to clear its ditches.

Herefordshire was also suffering from the national shortage of certified teachers and several women were persuaded to enter the classroom for the first time. Gladys Jones, the 24-year-old daughter of Mr and Mrs Jones of Wellington Court, became a cookery teacher, alarming her family by riding a motorbike to outlying schools to give classes. She had been quick to volunteer in 1914, training as a nurse in Cardiff before working in hospitals with convalescent soldiers. When in July the Women's Army Auxiliary Corps was formed, Gladys abandoned her motorbike and joined up.

Gladys Jones, pictured at work with a friend on the cabbage patch at Wellington Court, was quick to volunteer for active service.
(Photo: Barbara Perrin)

Gladys Jones trained as a VAD or Voluntary Aid Detachment as the individual nurses were known, providing field nursing at VAD hospitals for convalescing soldiers such as this one. Later she started teaching cookery, riding from school to school on her motorbike.
(Photos: Barbara Perrin)

The Education Committee, meanwhile, made belated attempts to improve slipping standards in schools by raising the salaries of its 491 elementary school teachers. The 186 heads and 305 assistant teachers saw their maximum pay rise to £180 a year, boosted by a war bonus of £8 a year, that April. Most 13-year-olds, however, had already left school to work on farms and in gardens, according to the Archdeaconry of Hereford's Voluntary Schools Association. Their Mr F.S. Horvin claimed that 'all lads of 12 who are intended for farm work were leaving [school] as rapidly as possible'.

The Education Committee's own figures confirmed that the illegal employment of school children was emptying classrooms. When attendance figures for 1916 were published they revealed 1,000 fewer children in school than in 1914. The labour leader Sidney Box rounded on the farmers: 'What have [they] done with regard to the education of the children of their labourers? They have begged the Minister of Education to allow them to take their children at an earlier age from school.'

The school rolls, which showed a drop from 12,459 in 1915 to 10,818 in 1916, caused the closure of Leinthall Starkes school while the rate of decline, 13.1% for 1915/16, was the worst in England or Wales. In Essex, the county with the second poorest figures, the fall was only 9.7% yet in July the committee was still reminding schools of their powers to close classrooms during the harvest so that children aged 12 and over could help on the farm. Like the county's war-weary farmers, the Education Committee was driven by deepening concerns that Britain was about to be starved into submission by its enemies.

At HWAC Councillor Langford reminded his colleagues that, next to the army, farmers were the most important class in the country. (Agriculture had its dangers too: 58-year old William Bowen of Woonton Ash, Lyonshall and 60-year-old Maurice Daly, lodging at 20 Blue School Street, Hereford were both fatally injured after falling from hayricks, Bowen at Lyonshall and Daly at Ox Farm, Whitecross.)

Earlier in the year the HWAC had appealed to the Land Agents' Society to help find fresh land for the plough. Several local agents offered their services including M.C. Connolly in Leominster, W.J. Davies in Hereford, F.J. Constable Curtis at Ganarew, J. Inglis on the Whitfield estate and John E. Hellyar Stooke in Hereford. Their initial report revealed 7,000 acres of new ground, prompting HWAC to approach private tractor owners to ask if they would plough this new farmland 'at a reasonable charge'.

As the county council considered buying its own tractors, the Board of Agriculture approached Fryer's Garage to run a small fleet taken from a national stock of 600 American motor ploughs and tractors. James Fryer was a former coal merchant with garages in Kington, Leominster and Hereford, behind the Green Dragon. New premises were opened in Widemarsh Street and George Butcher, former chauffeur to Brockhampton's Mrs Foster, was put in charge of finding drivers and maintaining the fleet. The government promised to pay 4 shillings a shift and farmers would pay the fuel and 17s 6d per acre.

But when it was announced that George Butcher was to work the machines on three eight-hour shifts, 24 hours a day using lights at night there was a storm of protest from farmers, not to night ploughing, which had never been attempted before, but to Sunday work. Many countrymen refused to plough on the Sabbath. Rural clergyman sought to reassure: Revd E.H. Archer-Shepherd from Avenbury Vicarage, Bromyard likened

George Butcher began his working days as a bicycle builder in Stonehouse, Gloucestershire before becoming chauffeur to Mrs Foster at Brockington. By 1916 he was working at Fryer's Garage, pictured here with his family and Mr Corbett-Winder in the driving seat. The two men were to become part of the record-breaking plough teams that toured the county.

Fryer's Garage in the 1920s. During the war the garage played a key role in providing and maintaining the machinery that ploughed up more 'milk meadows' than any other county.

the Sunday ploughmen to 'young men on a Sunday afternoon digging their Mothers' garden'. (It was, he suggested, better than leaving them 'hanging about the lanes in groups, waiting for Satan to find some mischief for idle hands'.) The Revd S. Cornish Watkins of Staunton on Arrow conceded that Sunday work was wrong under normal circumstances, but reminded his congregation: 'We who live in the country know well that there is only a limited time during which you could sow and reap.' Although Hubert Astley of Brinsop Court in a letter to the newspapers wondered why it was acceptable to light a fire and boil a kettle on Sundays, yet 'not do work to produce food', Burghill's John Fowler was adamant that Sunday remain a day of rest, pointing out that even the Minister of Munitions had announced that seven days' labour did not result in increased output.

That April the army reluctantly relieved 186 KSLI soldiers from military duties and sent them home to help with the ploughing, but a month earlier N.F. Bayliss from the Sunbeam Motor Company was already ploughing with a Bull tractor at Garnons while a Cockshutt Canadian plough was out on night work with Mr Corbett-Winder on the plough and Mr Gurney, chauffeur to a Mrs Rittner, at the wheel. (Corbett-Winder had started a garage, later Ravenhills, in Commercial Street, Hereford.) It soon became apparent to a group of farmers, gathered at Ruckhall to watch a tractor plough 25 acres of grassland, that the KSLI soldiers were a wasted effort: one farmer estimated that it would take even an experienced ploughman with a single furrow, horse-drawn plough four to five days to match the work done in one day with a mechanical plough.

Private tractors, organised by HWAC, were now turning the sward across the county. By the end of April there were around 21 tractors in action, 5 or 6 in private hands and 15 in the government fleet. A Titan arrived at Kington to work Mr Owen's land at Hergest Croft and another was dispatched to Wigmore. A Martin Motor tractor operated by Mr Cunningham from Westhide Court Farm was ploughing at Credenhill and a chain-steered Overtime at Leominster. Mr Passey at Ross was running a Mogul, which had already turned 26 acres at Mr Ratcliffe's Pigeon House, while an Overtime at Mr Cave's in Monkland ploughed 60 acres.

Several farmers who had booked a tractor still refused its use on Sundays as concerns grew over the loss of grazing sward and rich, milk meadows. A doubting district councillor, Mr Thorne, wondered if the machines would even last a month. The hardy little tractors, however, proved their worth and they were cheaper to maintain than a team of horses and a couple of labourers. HWAC continued to supply teams of ploughmen and horses for hire at 12 shillings a week per horse, but it was already apparent that the growl of the tractor engine heralded the end of the plough horse.

One of the breakthrough designs of 1917 was the four-furrow, self-lift La Crosse plough. George Butcher demonstrated the new plough, hitched to an Overtime tractor at Mrs Eli Smith's Pantall Farm in Sutton St Nicholas that summer as organisers of Hereford and Worcester's Two Counties Agriculture Show looked forward to further demonstrations at the annual show. However, having ignored a warning letter from Rowland Prothero (he had cautioned: 'There should be rigid economy in every possible quarter') they were in the final planning stages when the Minister of Munitions stepped in and summarily cancelled the show.

The Ministry, meanwhile, had been busy in Rotherwas: 'Men, money and munitions has come to be a sort of secular battlecry for the nation,' wrote a local reporter, given access to the new munitions factory at the start of the year. The author avoided identifying the location while imagining how such a 'well-considered factory' might operate. Free breakfasts would be served and an hour allocated for an 8d work dinner in an 8.5 hour working day. There would be dry clothing, a lady supervisor and a lady doctor. 'Were such a factory [to] be bounded by a salmon river,' conjectured the writer, 'are they careless of the fishing? No, the whole effluent of any chemical process is carefully self-consumed, and not allowed to enter the river.'

The promise of dry clothing was not born out in a critical report of the factory which was produced later for the Ministry of Munitions by Lilian Barker, superintendent at Woolwich. She noted the arrival of 65 new women workers, drenched from walking to the factory from the city. The factory secretary Mr Dunnett was forced to admit that there were no drying facilities. Worse still the women handling explosives in 'the fill' were, initially, given inadequate protection. The toxic nature of the explosives was well known. One letter to the newspapers complained about girls, drinking in city pubs encouraged by 'rumours that TNT poisoning is counteracted by alcohol'. (One inebriated worker was arrested after stealing a barometer from the nearby Wye Hotel: the 29-year-old told the court that he had mistaken it for a banjo.) Claims of drunken revelry were refuted by Ann Hutchings of Greenland Road who pointed out 'the sacrifice these noble girls are making, working in poisonous fumes and deadly powders'. Munitioneers, she said, were ignoring their looks and health, for King and country. Perhaps as a warning to local workers, a February edition of the *Hereford Times* covered the story of a group of Woolwich munitioneers who had been fined 15 shillings each for refusing to 'do work which might possibly cause discoloration to the skin'. The women were wise to be worried: TNT poisoning caused toxic jaundice, a potentially fatal condition that was, by 1916, classed as a notifiable disease.

By the time the young Annie Slade (she was under age) left her home at Pentre in the Rhondda and signed on at the factory, the girls were being given rudimentary protection. 'We had to wear masks on our faces, but my hair, it used to poke out, you know, and it all went green,' remembered Annie after the war. She was employed on the fill: 'You put the [explosive] powder in the shells in the stemming room. We had to work two weeks there and then on nights, two weeks on the mills and then back again.' The skin discolouration of the skin marked out the munitions workers in any crowd and soon earned them the nickname of 'Canary Girls'.

In March one 19-year-old Canary Girl called Florence Machin from Portfield Street was admitted to hospital. Discharged after two weeks, she was the first to be treated and over the next two years hospital beds were regularly occupied by sick factory workers. Eighteen-year-old Maggie Cullen from the hostel at 12 St Owen Street spent more than three months in hospital while 20-year-old Elsie Morris from Gwern y Fed Farm at Three Cocks was admitted in early December after being injured by a passing train. She was to lose her leg. The workers were drawn from across the country (hospital records listed home addresses as distant from Hereford as Hove, Liverpool, Southport and Killarney) and the sick included 13 cases of toxic jaundice, two of them fatal.

If the care of the workers was sometimes less than diligent, the management of several thousand feisty, and occasionally aggrieved, young women was inadequate. In one six month period 11 managers quit the factory and absentee rates frequently approached 10%. When workers' wages were summarily cut following the Easter and Whitsun holidays the management failed to handle the fallout. Production was interrupted as a group of workers walked out. The Hereford Trades Council, unable to represent the workers because of wartime legislation, later described the way the girls had been treated as a disgrace. Several had been forced to borrow money to pay for their lodgings.

During another strike, this time in October, one group of girls which included a Hereford woman, Ethel Eskins, and her married sister, continued working. But when they returned to Barrs Court Station on the works train they were met by a group of protesters that included the Barry girl Elsie Abel. There were shouts of 'cowards' and 'blacklegs' and in the ensuing scuffle, Ethel Eskins was struck on the head by a banner. The police seized Elsie Abel, then living at a hostel at 6 Maylord Street, and charged her with assault. Elsie pleaded not guilty, but the case, with Mayor Dymond as the adjudicating justice, was found. Elsie was given a month in prison. The National Union of Railwaymen denounced the sentence as unjust and vindictive and started a collection for her. The National Federation of Women's Workers declared their support for Elsie, pointing out that the factory prevented munitioneers airing grievances in a proper and constitutional way.

Elsie's imprisonment was raised in parliament by the Glasgow MP William Anderson, but locally the case provided many people with the opportunity to voice their resentment of the upstart factory girls. One, who signed her letter to the papers as 'whipped at school', declared: 'The truth is that in the class to which most factory girls belong, there is no discipline.' The author insisted that her own 17-year-old daughter was content to live quietly without the 'feverish craving for excitement' of the munitioneers. Revd A.B. Wynne-Wilson of St Nicholas Rectory spoke in support of the girls. 'It is well to remember that the new problems are due to war and that the newcomers are in the front line,' he wrote, suggesting, 'it is something less that patriotic to vilify them.' The clergyman Revd J. Meredith of Aylestone Hill disagreed: 'There is a serious moral peril threatening the young lives,' he warned, criticising the regular munitions Sunday night dances and advocating attractions of a more refined and uplifting nature.

The people of Ross appeared more welcoming to their munitions workers. Shortly before Christmas the Billeting Committee found homes for another 500 in the town and the girls arrived on 6 December to a warm reception at the Town Hall. They had to turn in early that night: the workers' train left at 5.30 every morning for its 45-minute run in to Rotherwas.

In Hereford meanwhile there was no public debate over the risks of having an explosives factory so close to the city. This was in spite of a disastrous explosion at Silvertown in London's East End that January which killed 70 people and destroyed 900 homes. (Eirene Duncombe from The Cloisters had organised a collection to raise money for the 25 East End cats rescued in its aftermath.) Nevertheless the Hereford Guardians were asked by Miss Profitt, secretary of the Advisory Committee for Women's Employment, to provide details on the number of beds that could be made instantly available in the event of an emergency. The Guardians had already relocated a group of their residents to the Wolverhampton and Worcester Workhouses in order to accommodate factory girls at their workhouse in Hereford. They would later secure Castle Pool House, which was converted into a munitions workers' hostel.

At the end of September the local newspapers carried the following notice: 'A large number of men and women will be shortly required for work on Munitions of War in the district. There will also be a number of openings for men with experience of control to be trained to act as foremen and supervisors, also for women to act in similar capacities.' As the number of workers rose from 600 in January to over 4,000 in December men such as the verger at Leominster church, Philip Johnson, resigned his position to take up work at the factory, as did Nellie Lambert of Edgar Street.

Life on the munitions did not suit everyone. That summer Robert Wilkins, a homesick worker from Suffolk, left the factory and, slipping into a field near the Three Horseshoes at Treville, cut his throat. Kingstone's Dr W.R. Foster was called out from his home at Haywood Lodge, but could do nothing to save the man's life.

There were also open tensions between the Irish and the English and Welsh workers. The opening of a new Catholic Girls' Club in Victoria Street and the activities of girls such as the Misses Smith, Kennedy and Campbell, who gave an impromptu performance of Irish jigs and 'songs from the Emerald Isle' at a social gathering in Hereford Town Hall, helped diffuse racial tensions, but they still simmered under the surface. (In

G.   R.

MINISTRY   OF   MUNITIONS.

A LARGE number of MEN and WOMEN will very shortly be REQUIRED for WORK on MUNITIONS of WAR in this District.

There will also be a number of Openings for Men with some experience of Control to be Trained to act as Foremen and Supervisors, also for Women to act in similar capacities.

A Special Appeal is made to unoccupied Persons

All applications should be made either personally or by letter to the Manager, Board of Trade Labour Exchange, Hereford.

An Officer will attend at the undermentioned places, who will give full particulars regarding Hours, Rates of Pay and Work, and will receive applications :—

LEOMINSTER—Old Labour Exchange, Broad-street, on Fridays,	2 to 4—5 to 7 p.m.
ROSS— Union Offices, Alton-street, on Thursdays,	3 to 5—5.30 to 7 p.m.
LEDBURY— Police Station, on Tuesdays,	3 to 5—6 to 8 p.m.
KINGTON— Rural District Council Offices, on Tuesdays,	2 to 4—5 to 7.30 p.m.
PRESTEIGNE— Post Office, on Wednesdays,	2 to 5 p.m.

The Hereford Labour Exchange will be Open Each Evening until 7 p.m., and on Saturdays from 2 to 6 p.m.

The advertisement for workers at Hereford's munitions factory placed in local papers on 30 September 2016.

June workers at one Hereford seed firm were taken aback to find an unexploded grenade in a consignment of grass seed supplied from Ireland.)

Matters came to a head on 2 August when a pitched battle broke out between Irish and English women at Barrs Court Station. The police restrained between 20 and 30 Irish women as the English workers caught the train for their night shift. Although the Irish girls managed to march back to their hostel at the Judge's Lodging House in Commercial Street that evening, between 50 and 60 were put on the train and sent home to Ireland the next day.

Factory workers continued to be held responsible for a variety of social problems. Alderman Wallis called on his council to light up Castle Green at night after witnessing (several times) scenes of shocking immorality there. 'It is scarcely safe for decent people to use the walk and where the mothers of these hussies were I do not know.' The new women's patrols were asked to speak to the young women who congregated at the taxi stands. 'Young fellows may like to joke with the girls, but they would never think of making one of them a wife,' wrote a complainant to the *Hereford Times*. The fact that the girls could afford to order a cab, and that there were women in police-like uniforms on the city streets, shocked the older generation, but for the likes of 19-year-old Sadie Lloyd and her sister Honor life was exciting. The daughters of an Almeley blacksmith, they were friends with Dolly and Beatrice Taylor. Beatrice had been working as a domestic for Marriotts the motoring family. Now all four were earning good money as munitioneers. They were proud of their work and if there was the occasional wolf whistle and shouts of 'Canaries' directed their way, they could smile, turn away and look forward to collecting their wages at the end of the week.

That summer saw them join several thousand munitions workers at the Edgar

Nellie Lambert was born at Edgar Street, Hereford in 1898, the second eldest of five children. When Nellie's father, a railwayman and former Boer War soldier, died in 1915 the 17-year-old Nellie managed to secure a job at the National Filling Factory to support the family. She would later recall queuing for food, performing in the factory choir and noting how the explosive powder turned her skin and hair yellow. It earned the munitioneers their nickname: the Canary Girls. (Photo: Fiona Penwarne)

Street football ground for an August Bank Holiday event which included a shell-filling demonstration by uniformed munitioneers under the watchful eye of factory supervisor, L.H. Ovens. Later that summer an afternoon of sport was organised by the factory's Mr. A.E. Whitehead in the grounds of the empty Rotherwas House, the former and now derelict home of the Lubienskis. Highlights of the event were captured on cine film and screened later at the Garrick Theatre. They showed the 'Melters' beating the 'Fillers' in a tug of war, the Hereford Workers' Boys' Band and prizes being presented by a recent arrival at the factory, Mrs Gaudet. This was the French-Canadian wife of the factory's newly appointed managing director, Colonel Frederick Mondelet Gaudet. Gaudet was a professional soldier and engineer who had commanded the first wave of Canadian soldiers in France in September 1915. When he fell ill he was withdrawn from active service and head-hunted by the Ministry of Munitions, which, drawing on his pre-war experience with ballistics and regular visits to Woolwich Arsenal, placed him in charge at Rotherwas.

The sport-starved Herefordshire public were gratified by such events. That autumn they were to be treated to a new social phenomenon: women's football. Munitions workers elsewhere were regularly putting on football matches, and thanks to city organiser H.J. Jones (he arranged several matches between Rotherwas and other munitions teams and from places such as Blaina and Ebbw Vale) women munitioneers played at the Edgar Street ground that October. Sadie and Honor Lloyd were picked for the match between factory teams described as 'M.I.D.' and 'S.D.', the former winning 3–0 after goals by M. Gammage and M. Meredith. Sadie sent a photo of herself and Honor to a friend in Craswall: 'We had this taken the day we played the men. Don't have a fright at the photo.'

One of the keenly contested events at the Rotherwas House sports day was a cigarette lighting race won by Miss Preedy. The cost of illegally lighting up at the factory, however, was dear: Ivy Smith of 174 Bodenham Road, Ellen Jane Corner of 9 Villa Street and Gertrude Jenkins of 26 Berrington Street were brought before Hereford magistrates after being found with matches inside the factory. Two girls

Nineteen-year-old Sarah 'Sadie' Jane Lloyd (bottom left) and her sister Honor (top right), pictured with two fellow munitioneers, were soon earning good money at the new National Filling Factory in Rotherwas.
(Photo: Tim Smith)

The National Filling factory 14 Stores team with Honor Lloyd, front centre, and Sadie Lloyd, top, 3rd from left. The girls brought women's football to Edgar Street. In 1921, the Football Association would ban women's matches from being played on its member clubs' grounds. (Photo: Tim Smith)

fainted when they were fined £5. After fining Katherine Redmond of 130 Widemarsh Street £2 for possession of a half cigarette and Keziah Beecham of 124 St Owen Street (it was her first week at work) £1, the magistrate Capt Morgan asked that the factory manager attend court so that the bench could ascertain what steps were being taken to make workers aware of the rules.

By the autumn, according to Col Clowes some of the munitions girls were switching to work for the new Land Army. The Herefordshire Women's War Agricultural Committee (HWWAC) reported that 137 girls were by then working on hops, fruit picking, thatching and forestry, including a gang of women employed in the woods at Lingen. (A women's forestry corps, controlled by the Timber Supply department of the Board of Trade, had been established in 1917.) Timber was in great demand for paper, construction and for fortifying the front line. The Craig Hill Steam Saw Works at Grosmont, for example, employed 30 people to process 20 to 30 tons of timber a week. (Production had been suddenly brought to a halt in May when a traction engine hauling timber to Pontrilas station broke down, blocking Town Farm Pitch for two days. The same evening a timber wagon descending Beech Hill Road with three horses ran out of control and ended up blocking the bridge at Hoaldalbert.)

The need to maintain men for forestry and farming was a source of frustration for tribunal members who continued to assess, and mostly allow, appeals against enlist-

The Women's Forestry Corps was active in several Herefordshire woodlands.
They were photographed here, stacking and sawing coppiced wood, by Alfred Watkins.
(Photo: Herefordshire Libraries)

ment. (Some feared the tribunals: farmer Daniel Meredith of Moraston, Bridstow killed himself with his shotgun in August, worried that his son's exemption was to be over-turned by the tribunal.) One member of Knighton's Tribunal, John Williams, called on his colleagues to strike in protest at the military authority's continued appeals against their decisions, and in Ledbury, Councillor Fred Ballard attacked 'the mad rate of taking labourers in all directions from the land'. He even accused the town tribunal of 'not doing their duty in retaining enough labour to produce food', prompting clerk Richard Homes to demand an apology. Ballard was unrepentant: 'It does appear to me that your tribunal has yet to learn that a man on the land can serve the country at the present moment just as much as a man in the trenches.' He was, he continued, 50% short of efficient labour and blamed overbearing military representatives who dominated the tribunals. He reserved his apology for the time taken to reply: 'My day begins early. I have been running nearly 70 head of dairy cattle with two girls and my letter writing is seldom finished till late at night.'

The Hereford Tribunal chairman James Corner was equally vexed when, during a January session, ten separate landowners appealed for 39-year-old land agent John E. Hellyar Stooke to be exempted. (The tribunal allowed exemption until June 24.) He also clashed with Revd F. Green who, as the temporary Master of the Golden Valley Hounds, supported an appeal for exemption for huntsman Leslie Tilbrook. Corner believed huntsmen should not be exempted, but Revd Green's persuasive argument that hunting encouraged the breeding of good horses for the front as well as helping the farmer won the day. Tilbrook was exempted for a further three months.

The issue of hunting in wartime continued to be debated. After Col Clowes offered the view that 'it would be a great pity to stop hunting' an anonymous contributor to the *Hereford Times* who signed himself 'Proprietor of Rotherwas' maintained that hunt horses for war work were 'a drop in the ocean of available supplies' and that the existence of 230 hunts was 'a disgrace to sport'. Hunting, he wrote, existed solely for 'the sport of a class who would be better employed in creative or productive occupations for the welfare of their fellow men'.

But South Herefordshire Hunt secretary Dudley Smith, repeating the view that money spent on hunting would otherwise be spent abroad, offered the view that 'hunting is the best training an officer, aye, and a civilian, can have for the sterner duties of war'.

He was supported by J. Wyndham Smith of Aramstone Court, Hoarwithy, who claimed hunting made 'men of our younger race by teaching them to ride boldly and fearlessly across country'. In the light of events unfolding on the Western Front, it was a naïve view, and that March Abergavenny farmers formally moved that 'in their opinion hunting should be done away with a year after the war'.

Meanwhile the tribunals continued, sending the landlord of Ledbury's Horse and Groom Hotel, George Parmee, to enlist and turning down an application for his workman to stay from farmer D.J. Thomas of Kivernoll Farm. Thomas turned to the bench and accused its chairman, W.G. Bankes, of bribing his farm men to go to war. 'I do not know a single man on your farm,' protested Banks to the disgruntled farmer.

At Ross it was the chairman Mr T. Preece's turn to lose his temper when the tribunal was asked to exempt gardener William Baskerville by his employer the Revd Theodore

Emmott, the vicar of Walford. Preece told the clergyman that it was perfectly scandalous for a minister of the Gospel to have so many servants 'in order to keep himself in luxury and ease'. Emmott, a widower, admitted employing seven servants including his butler, whom he described as a coloured man.

In October the Hereford Tribunal addressed the thorny issue of whether W.H. Pinniger of W.H. Greenland should be allowed to stay now that the former mayor, Mr Greenland, had more time to devote to his business. It was generously decided to give Pinniger leave to appeal again. Hereford's Rural Tribunal also allowed Sir Richard Rankin, the son of the late James Rankin, to keep his gardener, 31-year-old F.J. Smith who, Rankin told the bench, had assisted in the growing of eight to ten tons of potatoes and £35 worth of tomatoes at his Walterstone and Bryngwyn properties. Rankin successfully argued that Smith was better employed raising food locally than 'mending roads on Salisbury Plain'.

The Herefords were by now fighting in the Middle East and once again adding significantly to the lists of war dead and wounded. Having recovered from his injuries at Gallipoli, Percy Pritchard joined a Camel Corps fighting the Turks in Egypt. 'We were entrenched in various places all over the Sinai and used to ride all night, surround them [at] dawn and wipe them up,' he would later recall. As the troops reached the outskirts of Beersheba, Percy's application to join the Royal Flying Corps came through and he was sent to Cairo. 'That night my company was ordered to go round the back of the Turkish lines to draw them away from the Battle of Gaza. The Turks sent down a force and almost annihilated my company. I met some of the fellers that survived. They had an awful experience. Turks pinched their boots and marched them right the way up through Syria.'

In mid-April the newspapers had listed 14 killed, 68 wounded, 7 missing and 1 captured by the enemy, the dead including 22-year-old Pte Herman Izzard from Woodbine Cottage, Credenhill whose name had only recently been added to a roll of honour made from timber taken from *HMS Britannia* and inscribed with the names of the 50 Credenhill parish men who had enlisted. The shrine had been donated by Miss Ecroyd of Credenhill Court assisted by the vicar of Credenhill, Claud Lighton. (His personal ambition was to ensure that every wounded soldier, on their arrival at Hereford Station, be given a clean pocket handkerchief. It was a small gift, he allowed, but of greater value than flowers.) KSLI troops, meanwhile, benefited from a gift of 13,000 cigarettes collected for them by Mrs Mailes of Ivy House in Bewell Street. She had, at least, been able to bury her daughter following the Garrick fire, but most of the families of the fallen experienced a deep sadness at not being able to bury their dead. When in May the body of Cpl Walter Dallow from The Birches, Little Dewchurch was returned home – the 21-year-old machine gunner's body had been recovered from *HMS Donegal*, a hospital ship torpedoed and sunk in the English Channel – the whole village turned out for the funeral. Dallow's death was one of many. The 54-year-old Col Edward Lucas-Scudamore of Kentchurch Court had been killed in March. In April it was the turn of Pte Francis Horton, son of the former rector of Dewsall, Revd A.W. Horton. The actions of the Herefords in Palestine and Gaza resulted in the deaths of the son of the Leominster Town Clerk, Lt Grenville Levason; Thomas, the only son of Mr and

Mrs Charles Duffty of Chapel House, Brilley; and 21-year-old Pte Fred Low of Bullen, Ledbury. A widow, Mrs Kitty Wilmot living at Perrystone Towers, Old Gore near Ross was left grieving for her second son, Cecil, having lost her first son the year before. She was to lose her third son, Robert, before the year was out. (The mother of 11 children, Kitty had two other sons who were left permanently scarred by the wartime tragedy.)

So many men were killed that commanding officer Col Drage was prompted to record that his men 'met their death without flinching and their hardship and suffering without a murmur'. The anniversary of the outbreak of war that year had been a sober affair. As the suffragette Christabel Pankhurst attended the anniversary at Knighton, the names of the 108 'Hereford Heroes' killed during the previous three years were read out in the cathedral. By coincidence the same number of wounded arrived at Barrs Court station in the same week. The 'heroes of the Big Push', as the newspapers called them, were given tea and hospitality at the Soldiers' Rest before the less seriously injured were sent on to Ludlow and Church Stretton and the cot cases delivered to Hampton Grange and Beechwood by 30 volunteer ambulance men. The next month brought another 160 wounded men.

Other families had to cope with the news that their men had been taken prisoner of war. At the start of the year Mrs Mann at Woodhill, Ullingswick learned that her husband had been taken from the local newspapers as they listed him together with Pte G. Perkins from Ross, 22-year-old Pte Harry Francis of Eggleton, Pte W.J. Goodwin of Aston Ingham, Pte George Wall, L/Cpl George Millichap of Stockton, Pte Alfred Jones, the former 'boots' at the Crown Hotel, Hay, and Pte Percy J. Edmunds of 6 Clifford Street, Hereford. (He was said to be the first Herefordian to reach what the *Hereford Times* dubbed 'the capital of Hunland', Berlin.)

Prisoner of war Pte F. Davies from Brampton Street, Ross, meanwhile, was returned during an exchange of prisoners. Badly wounded in the face in 1914, his life had been saved by nursing nuns and his sanity, he said, by his Red Cross parcels. The fortnightly parcels were paid for by public subscription. His family at least knew where he was. Others such as Mrs Clarke of Brick House, Fownhope were left to post appeals in the press: 'I would be grateful for any information of my husband,' she wrote.

The injured Private Davies found himself living close to his former enemies when a group of German POWs were sent to the Ross municipal camping ground to work at the council's quarry at the rate of between 4d and 5d an hour. (British POWs, pointed out a bitter correspondent to the local press, were paid only 3d per day in Germany.)

Details such as these created little sympathy for the 33-year-old Greenlands furniture assistant, William Richardson of 11 Chandos Street when he appeared before Hereford City police court charged with being an absentee without leave. 'I am simply acting within my conscience before the Lord,' he told the magistrates' clerk, M.J.G. Scobie. Capt R.T. Hinckes from the recruiting authorities explained to the court that Richardson had been granted exemptions on condition that he did farm work but the conscientious objector, a fervent Plymouth Brother, refused. 'I could not willingly undertake work on the land, which would in principle, set free another man to do what I cannot.'

Maj G.J. Caldwell from the bench asked the defendant: 'Suppose I attacked you with a hatchet. Would you not hit back?'

'I may be tempted to do so, but according to the authorities of the Word of God I ought not to,' he replied, reminding the magistrates that they were not there to punish a man who, like himself, had a genuine objection to military service. The magistrates did not enjoy their lecture and Richardson was fined £2 and remanded to await a military escort. Richardson was compulsorily enlisted, but would refuse to put on a uniform. This led to his being court-martialled and sentenced to hard labour at Wormwood Scrubs.

The menace to food supplies from German U-boats had increased and a proclamation from King George on food economy (it was read out in public by bewigged, gowned and gloved town clerks) asked householders to reduce their consumption of bread by a third and abstain from using pastry. Every village school responded by hosting a parish meeting to look at ways of stepping up food production, especially in the vegetable garden.

That spring Hereford housewives had been startled to experience a potato famine. The absence of any potatoes in the city left Monkley's Stores in Bridge Street to advocate boiled peas ('No Food so Cheap and Nutritious') as a substitute. Now 63 tons of seed potatoes, purchased by the Education Committee, had been planted on school grounds while amateur gardeners had planted some of the £90 worth of seeds purchased by the HWWAC with Mrs Clowes at the helm. Under its president

'I am simply acting within my conscience before the Lord,' conscientious objector William Richardson told Hereford police court when arrested. Living in Chandos Street and worshipping as a Plymouth Brother, Richardson worked for Greenlands furniture store. He was sentenced to hard labour at Wormwood Scrubs prison. Later found to have a 'genuine' case, he was transferred to Dartmoor Prison. (Photo: Norman Richardson)

Eveline Cotterell, its members set out to stimulate better local food production. The members included Mrs A.W. Foster for Ross, Mrs Green in Wigmore, Miss Prescott Decie and Mrs G. Marshall at Breinton and Miss Lawson Walker and Miss Powell at Kington, and that autumn they arranged to offer prize money to the most productive amateur food growers. (The county council, meanwhile, had altered its policy of awarding prizes for 'fancy' cottage gardens; future awards would be given only for productivity.)

The Garway War Workers Association was especially active. Having found and killed four predatory foxes and crippled another two, the Association established allotments for its village school children. Ross Urban Council turned over three acres of land loaned to them by Mr W.H. Probert, while in Hereford Alderman Symonds mooted a plan to replace the flower borders in Castle Green with vegetable beds of carrots and beet. The idea was quietly put aside while the City Council commandeered the open space in front of the Girls' High School for allotments. The council also purchased ten tons of

When a potato 'famine' hit the city of Hereford Monkleys the grocery shop
in Bridge Street, Hereford recommended using boiled peas as a substitute.
(Photo: In Our Age/Herefordshire Lore)

King Edward, Arran Chief and President seed potatoes to be given away to allotment holders and corporation workers and started a special Wednesday fruit and vegetable market in the city. Small growers began sending in their own produce and as Barnsley and Davies auctioned the first lots Councillor Langford felt moved to declare that the county's cottage wives and children were now producing more food than many of the men. Villages including How Caple, Fownhope, Brockhampton, Hampton Bishop and three close to Weobley established special collection points for produce while 40 amateur growers in Bodenham proved so productive that their vicar, Revd F.W. Worsley had to hire a van to deliver the produce to the city market, raising £40 in the process.

As her husband John Arkwright worked on his poem *The Supreme Sacrifice* (set to music by the vicar of Colwall, Revd Charles Harris, it was to become the war anthem *O Valiant Hearts*) Mrs Arkwright gave £300 to a HWWAC fund to help gardeners grow more war food. Fred Cawley of Berrington Hall, who by now had lost two sons to the war, donated another £100. Miss Philips of Ivy Lodge, Hereford generously donated a load of manure to parishioners in All Saints while the Reverends C.A. Traherne and C.E. Whitcombe persuaded two professional gardeners, Mr Davies from Mrs Hewat's The Elms and Mr Brooks from Elmhirst, to assist with cultivating every scrap of wasteland in the city parish. Scudamore school's Mr Ryder promised to provide pupils to assist.

Kimbolton set up its own Wartime Garden Committee under Secretary Mr. F. Chandler; the vicar of Holmer, Revd H.E. Knight, initiated a parish programme to grow more food; at Wellington, parishioners ploughed up village land for potatoes; Humber school planted a war garden while Lucton parishioners received a donation of seeds from the Society for the Encouragement of Cultivating Cottage Gardens.

Ledbury Urban District Council, having abandoned plans to raise its own pigs (appeals for household swill had failed to produce sufficient feed), bought up supplies of seed potatoes for distribution to its cottagers; the Revd M.W. Mallinson of Woodlands agreed to advise on cultivation; and the town's Company of Volunteers under Mr C.H. Bastow planted up 22 gardens belonging to the wives of serving soldiers. (Seed potatoes at 3d a pound cost 1½d more than table potatoes and certain unscrupulous grocers including fruiterer Elizabeth Wright tried selling table potatoes as seed. Wright was fined for the deception.)

The Education Committee had taken up a suggestion of F.C. Collins from Ross to open a new cookery centre and Miss Mason and Miss Williams were soon offering useful advice on making vegetarian potted meat, maize meal bread and oatcakes, and demonstrating the use of the fireless box or hay box – 'newspapers may be used instead of hay'.

A cheese school was founded at Weobley, the committee retaining the services of its dairy instructresses who were paid £2 a week to run the county's two mobile cheese schools. County instructress Nellie Yeld received a bonus for her work from the committee after delivering a cheese course at The Knapp, Bridge Sollars, the home of Mr and Mrs Robert Blashill. In a bid to encourage more people to become dairymen and women the Education Committee adopted Shropshire's plan of sending older school children to work on dairy farms after school.

Even the county hedgerows were to be foraged for food. The secretary of the Herefordshire Herb Society, A.E. Chapman from Carfax, Aylestone Hill, appealed for fresh broom tips, laurel leaves, woodruff, balm, peppermint, comfrey, foxglove, colchicum bulbs, buckbean, yarrow, balm, henbane, belladonna, dried sloes and blackberries to be delivered to the Mitre Hotel. They were collected by Mr Andrews of Manor Farm, Bullingham and dispatched to London and Manchester. Chapman turned down any further donations of dried dandelion roots since he had received 2,500 pounds 'chiefly thanks to the fine exertions of Mrs R. Masefield in Ledbury'.

All this talk of food shortages exasperated some. Dorothy Stopford Evill of St Martin's Vicarage wrote to the press after receiving a letter from her brother who, with the East African Expeditionary Force, had recently enjoyed his first fresh vegetables in 15 months. 'I can't help feeling that if some people would realise the hardships which our soldiers are undergoing ... they would be more willing to tighten their belts, to cease grumbling at war bread, and to thank God and our Navy that we had those rations left us.' For A.J. Detheridge of Kewstone House, Moorfields, the focus for food was firmly on river fish. He maintained that tons of perch, dace, chub, pike and even trout, grayling and salmon could be taken from the river 'without doing harm to the sporting rights'. The Wye Conservators were resistant to the idea although T.J. Stokes of Hay wrote to the local press enthusiastically encouraging the adoption: he was already concerned about the soaring cost of rabbit – 'the staple foods of the poor' – then fetching 4/4d a pair. The poor were also on the mind of Revd S. Cornish Watkins, who wondered where all the starlings, which formerly, 'like the poor were always with us', had gone. If the starlings had fled the vicarage at Staunton on Arrow, the poor were still very much present.

At the start of the year the Hereford Union, City Asylum and Dore Union Guardians had put out their usual tenders for food ('meat for three months; new milk for 12 months') and services ('hearse to Burghill as per journey'). But by March the Weobley and Dore Board had introduced meatless days at the workhouse and were soon reconsidering the 10.5lbs weekly bread allocation that was allowed for each tramp. After an intervention from John Cotterell – 'I think we must knock some of that off' – the ration was reduced to 6 ounces per meal with 12.5 ounces of cheese. Other economies were to follow, one workhouse substituting herrings for meat once a week, as Hereford Market imposed its own 'meatless Wednesdays' on customers. The average farmer, however, was more a salmon than a herring man and these 'market ordinaries' triggered an immediate increase in the price of salmon of 7d per pound.

The lack of meat worried Hereford Councillor Ballard who was concerned that many schoolchildren were becoming malnourished, while in Eastnor the village women followed the example of a group of mothers at Much Marcle who had clubbed together to prepare school meals for their 34 schoolchildren. There was no doubt that people were feeling the pinch, especially in Ledbury: the rector took to his pulpit to condemn the increasingly common practice of placing buttons in the offertory box.

Hereford's city fathers, meanwhile, were concerned about the lack of entertainment available to soldiers milling about the streets on leave and munitioneers walking around after their work was done. (A blast of wintery weather earlier in the year, which saw Leominster slip under eight inches of snow, provided plenty of entertainment at Barrs Court Station when munitions girls waiting for the works train engaged in a pitched snowball fight with servicemen waiting for their own train.) Hereford Corporation had introduced Sunday winter opening at the library and museum although patrons complained that the absence of heating left the facilities too cold to enjoy such recent exhibits as an unexploded German bomb, donated by David Davies of Eign Street. (The library was once again closed on Sundays at the start of the summer in anticipation of its patrons preferring more outdoor recreation.)

To counter the lack of entertainment a soldiers' club was started up at the Assembly Room in the Shirehall. It opened with a performance by the Wye Glee Singers and a string of songs from the Savoy quartet composed of Mr Batey and Mr Herbert and the Misses Nash and White. The club offered buffet and billiards (the tables provided by H.P. Bulmer) every evening from 6 to 10pm.

A Girls' Club was opened at 25 High Town by the Hereford Diocese, 'a commodious place of several rooms, artistically decorated', according to the *Hereford Times*. Its 100 members were expected to pay 10 shillings a year to join. Another club and hostel for factory girls was opened by Dean Leigh's niece Lady Jersey at Wilson Chambers in Commercial Street. (The dean had repeatedly called for more hostels to be provided in addition to the six or seven then operating in Hereford.) Lady Jersey took the opportunity at the opening to remind people of the need to care for the welfare of the munitions girls. Even the bishop was moved to admire their work. Commending the noble way in which women were performing 'national patriotic work', he predicted that the girls who 'undoubtedly put their sex in a different position to the life of the nation' might help bring about the complete emancipation of women. It was a telling observation for an elderly man, a teenager at the time of the Irish famine, observing in his twilight years some of the most radical social changes the city had ever seen.

The Hereford dean, meanwhile, had rushed off to raise funds towards the £800 cost of providing another meeting place, the Central Club, situated at the corner of St Peters Square and Offa Street. Provided by the Recreation Advisory Committee on Women's War Employments (Industrial), the club with its reading room, snuggery and refreshment rooms, all 'chastely but inexpensively furnished', according to the *Hereford Times*, was expected to attract a substantial donation from the government.

Sunday night for the off-duty munitioneer and soldier alike remained a dull affair for now, and yet when the Garrick Theatre applied to put on films mostly for munitioneers on Sunday nights Hereford magistrates refused a licence. There was a storm of protest over the decision. Even the conservative *Hereford Times* declared in a leader: 'We should ten times prefer to see Sunday evening concerts in every available hall than that these young girls should be compelled to wander aimlessly about the deserted streets during the coming winter.' The magistrates eventually bowed to public pressure and reversed their decision. When proposals were put forward for the creation of a new 270-seat picture house to be opened in a former Salvation Army hall on St Owen Street, they approved that too. The decision did not please everyone. Councillor Merrick, who advocated that film programmes be subject to 'effective censorship', claimed that a lot of juvenile offences could be attributed to crime films.

No one, however, could blame the Hollywood movies for the shocking murder of chip girl Freda Wilson. She had been serving in her father's shop, Wilson's Fish and Chips, next to the Fleece in St Owen Street when a Liverpudlian soldier walked in and, taking a carbine from under his greatcoat, shot her in the chest at point blank range. Twenty-six-year-old Freda was rushed upstairs, but died three hours later. It transpired that the soldier, Pte Thomas Breen, had developed an obsession for Freda, which she had not reciprocated, while billeted with the Wilson family. After the shooting he calmly gave himself up to police.

The Hereford Hospital, meanwhile, had taken the unprecedented step of advertising the services of its new £320 a year unit for the treatment of venereal disease: the City Lunatic Asylum had reported having dealt with several cases of syphilis amongst the 700 people it treated the previous year. The new year, however, brought a new health threat: pneumonia. February 1917 had been the coldest on record for 22 years. It killed casual labourer George Beavan who died of exposure in a barn at Saddlebow Farm, Orcop, and triggered an alarming rise in deaths at the soldiers' barracks in Park Hall Camp, Oswestry and Prees Heath Camp, Whitchurch, Shropshire. In Hereford a new 40-bed hospital, opened at Holbrook House as an annex to the Hampton Grange VAD Hospital under Commandant E. Brenda Lee, was soon dealing not only with wounded soldiers, but soldiers with pneumonia. That spring mourners had packed the little church of St Margaret's at Michaelchurch Escley for the funeral of Pte A.E. Howard, an 18-year-old from Alma House who had died of pneumonia at the Prees Heath Camp. After reports that 17 men had died, 12 from pneumonia, in a single week at the camps, Hereford's MP William Hewins raised the matter in parliament bringing to the government's attention the deaths of several other young men from Kingsthorne, Much Dewchurch, Grafton, Sollars Hope, Fawley and Brockhampton. A number of Hereford councillors, Aldermen Wallis and Greenland among them, avoided criticising the officer in charge, Col Symonds-Taylor, but repeated the view that the 'war babies', boys forced to enlist while unfit for service, had fallen ill because of a regime of hard, physical exercise on an empty stomach.

As the year went by austerity bit deeper than ever and the quantity, quality and cost of food was on everyone's mind. Labour leader Sidney Box claimed that prices had risen by 104% since the war began amidst rumours that Herefordshire was paying more for food than its neighbouring counties. It prompted the new mayor Councillor Dymond to go on a fact-finding mission. 'The allegations are untrue,' he concluded.

Box also attacked employers and financiers who, he said, were profiting from the war. He cited Strathmore Rubber Company (shares up by 30%), Frederick Leyland (88%) and the Projectile Company (550%). 'No wonder some foster the war,' he wrote in a letter to the press.

In order to conserve wheat supplies the millers' offal, the coarser parts of the grain, were now to be added to bread flour instead of being sent for animal feed. A Saville Row doctor declared the new bread was far superior to the old white loaf. 'White bread is a delusion and a snare,' he claimed in what was transparently a planted letter to the local newspapers 'and when used as the principal item in one's diet starves the body and nerves and tends to undermine the digestion.' 'Not so', growled miller Alfred Watkins whose flour mill in Friar Street was about to be requisitioned by the government: 'The instinct of the people to select by preference white bread has been a perfectly sound one.'

The grain crisis prompted the temperance Strength of Britain Movement to advocate diverting barley sales away from the brewers. Town pubs had already been stopped from serving drinks after 9pm (Ethel Hall and Annie Sheen were fined £1 each for late drinking, 9.05pm, at The Mitre) while Garway's War Workers Association bemoaned the fact that their pubs remained open until 10pm allowing labourers to spend money they could ill afford.

Temperance supporters, Alderman Wallis among them, helped organise an open-air city rally aimed at persuading young soldiers to avoid the 'wet huts' (where alcohol was served) and patronise the dry ones such as those run by the YMCA. Rest huts, many supported by local organisations, played an important role on the front line: in July Revd J.W. Kettle returned from France to explain their role to his fellow Baptists at the Broad

Street church. (Kettle also revealed the growing conviction among the soldiers he met that this war would never be brought to an end by fighting.)

By now a coffee stall and temperance café had opened at the market staffed by Mrs A.E. Butterworth of Aylestone Hill, Miss R. Marrillier of Pengrove Road and Miss A.M. King of Hafod Mount. It was the brainchild of Dean Leigh, who warned wives and mothers of the dangers of drink at a city interdenominational meeting: 'Women should do their best by making their homes as attractive as possible,' he said, reminding his listeners that giving the homecoming soldier or sailor a welcoming drink risked entangling them in 'the meshes of undesirable female acquaintances. When beer comes before bread, then the people perish.'

It was not the only danger facing people. According to the county surveyor, motor traffic had fallen since the start of the war. It fell further in the summer when the Minister of Munitions banned the use of 'holiday petrol': Connelly's Garage at Kington was fined £3 for taking the wedding party of Frank Jones of Burcher Farm, Titley to Hereford. However, heavy haulage, especially of timber, had risen as had the county council's underspend on Herefordshire's 501 miles of road. The money spent had fallen to £40 3s per mile on its 463 miles of rural roads compared with £79 3s before the war and £154 3s per mile on urban roads compared with £193 5s.

Poor roads did not improve standards of driving: the assistant manager at one of the factory canteens was killed when his motorcycle left the road, and farmer Henry Gwilliam was pitched into the road at Harewood End when an army instructor drove through the village so fast it frightened Gwilliam's horses. Meanwhile a 63-year-old corporation worker, James Jones of Catherine Street, had an unfortunate accident when his foot was crushed by a steam roller as he was repairing the road on Aylestone Hill. He died shortly afterwards.

Another threat to life and limb came from the air. Leominster people were reported to have had their first glimpse of an aircraft, which mysteriously passed over the town that summer, dropping a package at Oaklands near Ysciog. (The parcel, containing tins of what were thought to be Swiss soup cubes, was handed over to the Brecon police.) Meanwhile Florence Austins, the daughter of the Commercial Street skin yard owner G.E. Herron, arrived at Barrs Court Station to welcome home her husband, Andrew, on leave. Only then did she learn the former Bridge Street ironmongery assistant had become the second county victim of an air attack. The 31-year-old, who had been serving as an air mechanic on kite balloons at Felixstowe, had been killed during an air raid on the town. It persuaded the local authorities to devise procedures for sounding an air-raid warning in the case of attack. Householders were advised to stay indoors and go to their cellar – if they possessed one.

Christmas 1917 was a quiet, sombre affair. The thousands of munitioneers had left for home – only 5 of the 28 factory workers staying at the Girls' Hostel in Wilson Chambers remained in Hereford. As if anticipating the arrival of the Americans in France, the Women's Welfare Club in St Owen Street hosted a film show and an 'American Surprise' party for those left behind. There was even roast beef to be had at the Hereford Workhouse.

Chapter 6

1918

As the number of munitioneers rose towards a peak of 5,864 the county was burdened beneath its heaviest snowfall in 37 years. Even the news that the Americans were to join the war failed to lift people's spirits. The end of the war, however, was in sight.

Life on the home front could be hard for Herefordshire's war widows. After her soldier husband was killed on the front line, Annie Strangwood and her three children were faced with eviction from their home at 9 Cranes Lane, Leominster. Annie's landlady, Mary Wilkes, had applied for an eviction order from Leominster Borough police court after Annie fell into arrears of 9 shillings. Annie explained that, living on a pension of £1 6s 3d and her eldest child's earnings of 8 shillings a week, she had spent her rent money on children's shoes.

Wilkes' solicitor discreetly reminded the court that, while there was sympathy for widow Strangwood's circumstances, the bench was obliged to judge the matter from a business point of view. He added that his client's rent collector, who called ten days after Annie's husband's death the previous October, had been physically threatened by Annie's sister. She told him: 'If you say much more I will put you over the wall.' The court refused the application and expressed the hope that a different rent collector would be employed in future.

Life was little better for the four children of Pte Percy Hayton, killed in France in March 1917. Since the soldier's death, his wife Daisy had struggled to support their three teenage children, his mistress Mary Bernstein and her child by him, at the family home, 4 Gorsty Villas in Tupsley.

Daisy worked on the munitions and her circumstances only came to light when Mary fell out with her host and complained to the police. Mary had been born in Metz, which made her a German national. She had become pregnant by Percy, a bookmaker, while working as a typist in Switzerland. Percy had persuaded his wife to take Mary and their child in: 'I cannot afford to keep two family homes,' he told Daisy.

Daisy now found herself charged with knowingly harbouring an alien for two years. She was fined £5. Mary Bernstein suffered a far worse fate. She was separated from her child and deported to Germany, the magistrates telling Mary that her infant would be better looked after in England. What happened to the child or Mary, a Jewish woman in a nation that was soon to wage war on its Jewish citizens, remains unknown.

The circumstances of war forced many women to postpone starting a family and the county's new Medical Officer for Health, Dr Dryburgh Gold, found that the Herefordshire birth rate had sunk to its lowest level on record having fallen to 17.6% per 1,000. The news led to a disturbing encounter for Marguerite Jenin-Claud, a French woman living in Little Birch. She was walking through Hereford when a man suddenly seized her by the arm. 'Why don't you have a baby?' he demanded to know. 'The tragedy in my life is that I have no child,' Marguerite Jenin-Claud wrote in a letter to the newspapers.

At Wellington Court, meanwhile, the Jones family feared for their future as their last son Rowland went to war. Rowland had enlisted with the fledgling Royal Air Force – an advertisement in the local press, sponsored by Hereford grocer Gurney's, had appealed for 'aviators and pilots from 17 years and 11 months: apply Hereford Recruiting Office'. As Rowland left the family home, his sister Gladys, now serving with the Women's Army Auxiliary Corps, took the Channel ferry to Boulogne where she would assist in the soldiers'

The youngest of the Jones boys at Wellington Court, Rowland had been taken out of school to work the farm when his older brothers went off to war. Now it was his turn. He signed up with the fledgling Royal Air Force. (Photo: Barbara Perrin)

rest camps for the rest of the war. (In the event, all the family would return home safely.)

Farmers like the Jones family were as short of labour as ever. In early January one South Herefordshire farmer advertised: 'Wanted for Trelasdee, under waggoner and shepherd, good wages and privileges to good man; cottages provided.' His was one of 30 similar advertisements. The 'good wages' were to rise in June to 31 shillings for a 48-hour winter week and 56-hour summer week with 8d an hour overtime. By then the local workforce had been boosted by a pool of 460 skilled and 250 unskilled soldiers and no less than 1,300 women. The extra workers were needed to meet the government's aim of putting an additional 40,000 acres, or 50% of the county's existing grassland, to the plough. As the county's North and South Farmers' Unions came together to form one body, Herefordshire was divided into three districts: Hereford, Weobley, Ledbury and

After the deaths of so many men, the government formed the Women's Auxiliary Army in 1917 to carry out office, canteen, transport and stores work. Photos from Gladys Jones' album show her colleagues in their smart new uniforms. (Leather gloves signified drivers.) Gladys quit her work as a teacher and joined the transport division. She was eventually posted to France.
(Photos: Barbara Perrin)

A horse-drawn plough and its team near Longtown.
While protests over plans to plough on the Sabbath were ignored by the new mechanical
ploughing teams, many farmers still refused to allow the plough out on a Sunday.
(Photo: Winnie Reece)

Bredwardine; Ross, Whitchurch and Dore; and Leominster, Kington, Wigmore and Bromyard. Each was allocated a target acreage for ploughing.

The work was to be shared between teams of horses and the estimated 28 tractors operating in the county that February. It was not without problems. In May a Pte Rimmer was killed after being caught in the flywheel of one of the mechanical units. And with so much dairy pastureland and what one farmer described as 'good milk meadows' under threat, conflict between farmers and officials was inevitable. As soon as the 1918 Cultivation of Lands Order was published several hill farmers lodged appeals against their allocation of land to go under the plough. The effect of ploughing so much land and the continued felling of so many woodlands (timber hauliers in the west were warned by Hay District Council about the dangers posed by the great stacks of felled timber by the roadsides) would have a significant impact on the landscape, the wildlife and farmers' pockets.

One objector to the ploughing was Grosmont farmer Henry Partridge of Pant-y-Seal farm. He resisted an official order to plough Lower Meadow, which he described as one of the best butter fields in the county, and instead offered Little Oak Meadow, insisting that 'no man with any experience of river meadows would have recommended the committee to break up such a piece as the Lower Meadow.' But ploughing went ahead and Partridge was summoned to court for refusing the order despite, as he claimed, losing £100 worth of hay from Lower Meadow. (Such a crop, he pointed out, 'is badly wanted by the Army'.)

As if to confirm Henry Partridge's opinion of the authorities, John Cotterell attacked the HWAC that October, accusing it of employing men who were incompetent. By

OVERTIME

The British Champion.

The "Overtime" Tractor which holds the Championship Shield.

THE "OVERTIME" TRACTOR in the Hereford unit has scored a great success. Driver S. W. Powell and Ploughman J. G. H. Wall have succeeded in gaining the blue ribbon of all British Government tractor ploughing units by winning the British Championship Shield for the best month's work. They ploughed 154 acres in the four weeks ending March 8th. At Chequers Court on Sunday, April 14th, they were presented to Sir Arthur Lee, who handed them the Championship Shield. Congratulations to the Hereford unit under the able management of Mr. G. H. Butcher, the Hereford County tractor representative.

This is the way to win the war—the "Overtime" way. Plough more land, cultivate it quicker and at the right time. That is what you can do with an "Overtime" always ready for work on your farm. There is always a job for the "Overtime" all the year round. Write to-day for a copy of "Farmers' Reports," and read what "Overtime" owners can do with their tractor. Then order your "Overtime" Farm Tractor, 24-h.p. Paraffin.

Now is Your Opportunity.   Order an "OVERTIME" To-day.

NEW PRICE £292 5s.

The Overtime Farm Tractor Co., 124, Minories, London, E.1.

With the mechanical ploughs covering in a day what had taken horse-drawn ploughs four to five days, Herefordshire saw more land ploughed, and more cheaply, than any other county. 'This is the way to win the war,' wrote a correspondent in *Modern Farming* magazine.
(Photo: Glen Butcher)

Herefordshire's old woodlands were decimated by wartime demands. Timber was required for everything from pit props to trench works and woodlands such as this, now known as Queens Wood, Dinmore, suffered. (Photo: Michael Griffith)

then another 23,000 acres had been put to the plough and Cotterell declared that in the Weobley district 'the amount of unsuitable land that had been ploughed up was utterly disgraceful'.

The loss of livestock grazing was discussed by delegates attending the Council of Sanitary Institute's annual conference held in Hereford in May. The county surveyor, G.H. Jack, favoured the plough. Much of the county, he told delegates, was suffering from 50 years of neglect, pointing out that the 74,402 country people who occupied around half a million acres of rural Herefordshire needed well-drained low land, with all its brooks and ditches cleaned out and flowing fast. But many farmers remained unconvinced and when the September harvest was delayed by ten days of continuous rain, several wondered whether they might receive compensation from the government after having suffered a poor harvest and losing their traditional sward.

Ploughing with horses had carried on through the spring and into early summer, prizes of two guineas each being distributed by benefactor Harold Barnett of Burghill to the men who ploughed the largest acreage in the Hereford district (George Gibbons of Church House Farm, Weston Beggard) and Ross district (Alf Brookes of Hendre, Glewstone and joint winner Meredith Pritchard of Penedree, Longtown).

The tractor ploughs continued to attract interest. Fryer's had started advertising its own Fordson tractors at £250 – 'displaces Three or Four horses' – while in January George Butcher offered two tractors to Kington's War Agricultural Committee. He asked for a volunteer 'or a poor man who might receive 10 shillings expenses' to act as organiser, to which Kington's Mr Philpin replied that such a post would require 50 shillings at least a week. Butcher accused Kington's committee of a lack of patriotism and the debacle triggered a debate at HWAC over the costings of the government tractor units which now comprised 11 tractors, an engineer who was paid £5 a week, and two mechanics. Farmers were charged 20 shillings per acre although the actual cost was put at 25s 3d. Running the Herefordshire unit were R.P. Ravenhill as engineer, Eric Williams as supervisor, A.R. Croome as supplier and Herbert Minton as mechanic.

It was a winning team. That March Herefordshire broke the record for the greatest acreage ploughed, Messrs S.W. Powell and J.G.H. Wall having managed 61 acres in a week. It prompted George Butcher, now invested with one of the earliest OBEs awarded for services to agriculture, to declare Herefordshire the premier county for government ploughing. The county was still in the lead for the British Motor Ploughing Championships that June when Powell and Wall turned over 164 acres, 33 more than their rivals in the Holland Division in Lincolnshire. By the end of 1918 Herefordshire had put more acres to the plough, and more cheaply, than anywhere else in England or Wales.

Farmers were also making the most of a new source of labour: German prisoners of war (POWs). In February plans had been announced to turn part of the Weobley Workhouse into accommodation for 40 POWs. (Guardian Board member Col Clowes was moved to recommend the closure of the whole workhouse; he did not elaborate on what should be done with the 12 tramps still in residence.) Leominster and Ledbury Workhouses also agreed to billet similar numbers of POWs. By then the government had announced its intention to abolish the board of guardians for each workhouse, causing Ledbury board member J.C. Davies to attack the proposals and voice his opposition to a local plan to purchase a dwelling for a children's home. It was, he said, all 'a Socialist idea and a humbug'.

For the most part, the farmers and the POWs rubbed along amicably despite the occasional disagreement. In March, farmworkers at Kingsland Station had to intervene when two aliens, Hungarian Andre Weisz and Bohemian Wenzel Hammerl started fighting each other while unloading wagons. In August Jean Dian, classified as an enemy alien being a German national living in Britain at the outbreak of the war, was arrested for having wandered more than five miles from his place of residence in Leominster, and in October Ross farmers were asked to be less generous with their POWs: the farmers were said to be giving the men food at work, allowing the prisoners to hoard their government-supplied midday rations for a night-time feast. It was a custom, reported one newspaper, to which the German was addicted.

But if times were hard, there was still plenty of cash in circulation. When Herefordshire soldier Stephen Clifford of Eign Road was taken to court for stealing a purse from horse dealer Thomas Fury at the Market Tavern (he was found not guilty), Fury put the purse's contents at 'about £45', or nearly eight times the weekly wage of the average labourer. Such revelations fuelled resentment between those on the war front and those on the home front. 'After two years' work in France I am disgusted by the number of men of military age, notably of the farmer class, still exempt from military service,' wrote one clergyman that July.

Fury's purse snatch was part of a countywide crime wave, according to magistrate James Corner. At the Easter quarter sessions he had revealed what he described as a lamentable increase in crime, the number of lesser offences rising from 76 in 1915 to 109 in 1917, while indictable offences had almost doubled to 1,466. In all, 28 gaol sentences had been handed down. One was to 38-year-old ex-soldier, now farm labourer, Michael McCarthy from Presteigne, arrested in Hereford after being seen wearing medals which were not his own. McCarthy was sentenced to a month's hard labour.

In 1918, as in 1917, many of those sent to prison were young men and women employed at the munitions factory. In April, as a group of munitions workers performed their own Munitions Review at the Kemble Theatre, munitioneer Mary Elizabeth Watkins of 30 Caradoc Street, Pentwyn, Abersychan was left weeping in the dock as magistrates sent her to prison. Mary had been under age when she first secured work at the factory. When her real age was discovered the 16-year-old was laid off until her next birthday. She was then re-engaged that January and placed in lodgings at the Castle Pool House hostel. Mary gave up her job in late March but a week later asked the lady superintendent Mrs McTurk if she could be re-employed. The superintendent refused and the impoverished girl pinched a pay slip from her lodging mate, Edith Mayo, drawing Edith's week's pay of £3 1s 10d.

Mary pleaded not guilty to stealing the money, but having listened to evidence from assistant lady superintendent Miss Turner, staff supervisor Mr A.E. Whitehead, wages

In April local munitions girls line up on stage at the Kemble Theatre for their own Munitions review. There were now 2,724 women at the factory, a number set to rise to nearly 4,000. (Photo: In Our Age / Herefordshire Lore)

clerk Miss E.A. Place, worker Charlotte M. Watts, clerk Nellie Williams and Castle House Hostel superintendent Mabel Ann Cox, the magistrates found her guilty. Mary burst into tears as superintendent Weaver told the court: 'She has a good character at home but since coming to Hereford has transgressed.' The 17-year-old was sent to prison for a month.

A common crime at the factory was registering a friend as being present when they had already left – 'clocking off' for someone else. Former miner Joe Connell, aged 22, and his mate Ernie Chapman were brought to court after Connell was caught clocking off Chapman. Both men lodged with a Mrs Evans in Park Street and Chapman had already arrived back home at the time of the offence. Connell and Chapman were both sent to prison for three months on a charge of defrauding the Ministry of Munitions of Chapman's day-shift money, amounting to 4s 8d.

Hereford magistrates dismissed a similar case of conspiracy against two munitions workers, 21-year-old Joe Davies and 22-year-old Thomas Price. Davies, a Somme veteran, had been hit and injured by a trolley at the factory and returned home early. Price clocked Davies' card later and was accused of defrauding the Minister of Munitions of the shift money, 4s 1½d.

Most factory cases, however, involved the illegal possession of smoking materials. In May those charged included William Newton of Bewell Street (10 cigarettes, £2 fine), Benjamin Joseph Cole of Haywood Lodge Cottage (cigarette papers and a pound of tobacco, £2) and Arthur Stubbs of 10 Victoria Street (box of matches, one month imprisonment). When Alice Cooper of 3 Foley Street was brought before the bench accused of having a single match caught in the fold of a roll of tape, she went to the expense of hiring a solicitor, Mr Matthews. He told the court she was innocent of the match's existence and accepted a £1 fine on her behalf.

The exemplary prosecution of factory workers sometimes involved very minor thefts. In November lavatory attendant Maria Pitts was charged with stealing a roller towel worth 3s 6d. She protested that she had brought her own towel to work so that she could have a bath, but evidence from factory constables Margaret Campion, Hilda Peploe and Miss Dover, under their supervisor Miss Evelyn Deane, saw Maria found guilty. She was fined £5.

The behaviour of munitioneers off duty continued to be a cause for concern to members of the voluntary Women's Patrol. Under their leader Lady Alice Butler, the sometimes overzealous women, all aged over 25, devoted at least two hours a week to patrolling in pairs between 8pm and 10.30pm. Butler reported through her solicitor to the Hereford Brewster Sessions in March on their inspection of two Hereford city public houses, the Exchange and the municipal-owned Number 10 in Widemarsh Street where 20 girls were seen to be 'rollicking and cheerful'. Miss Blanche Acton Redwood from the bishop's committee charged with looking after munitions women corroborated Lady Butler's observations. Visiting the Raven six months earlier she found girls 'very nearly drunk' and sitting on soldiers' knees.

After hearing several cases involving factory workers, the Hereford magistrates called the factory's Medical Officer of Health, Dr Castellain, before them to explain the girls' behaviour. Dr Castellain assured the court that the management did all in their powers to keep the girls in what he described as 'a high state of mental control'. Many workers, however, continued to believe that alcohol was good for them despite advice to the contrary issued by the factory's welfare department.

Around the same time the newly enthroned Bishop Henson met a large contingent of factory workers together with their managing director, Col Gaudet, to share his views on the war 'against moral evil'. In February the 55-year-old Hensley Henson had replaced Bishop Percival, now living out the final months of his life at Oxford. Henson had been appointed by Prime Minister David Lloyd George despite objections to his liberal views from local churchmen and the Archbishop of Canterbury. Speaking to the factory women, the bishop took the old-fashioned view and commended the grace of chastity, condemning the evils of prostitution and asking his listeners to dip in their pockets to support The Haven Maternity Home. In 1917 this city home had accommodated 42 girls, 10 of them from the factory.

The bishop had his detractors. Sharing the platform with him was a Miss Higson, one of the new breed of women who felt confident enough to challenge some of the old-fashioned views. She pointedly mentioned modern society's double standards when it came to morality, one for men and another for women. What was needed, she suggested, was not censure but comradeship.

Herefordshire's pioneering working women continued to experience prejudice. Two Land Army women complained to the local papers: 'Until we came here we always received due respect … but we are discouraged by the disparaging remarks that are made to us.' Such attitudes were highlighted by the attempted arrest of two Land Army women, Mrs Daphne Perkins and Mrs Florence Price, by Miss Rosamond Marillier that May. Rosamond was a respectable 61-year-old spinster who lived with her sister at Brynmawr, 8 Grove Road, Hereford. She was the superintendent at Dean Leigh's Temperance Market café, the daughter of the late Revd J.F. Marillier, vicar of Much Dewchurch and sister to Frank Marillier, a technician with the GWR and the man credited for the ground-breaking design of the railway ambulance carriages that saved the lives of so many wounded soldiers as they were ferried back from France. Rosamond was also a member of the women's patrol and it was in that capacity that she stopped Mrs Perkins and Mrs Price in Hereford on the grounds that they were drunk. Notwithstanding Rosamond's social position, the two ladies, both former munitions workers, refused to go quietly and Marillier tried to arrest them. Eventually the two women agreed to accompany her to Hereford police station where Miss Marillier demanded that they be detained in the cells overnight. The police refused.

Mrs Perkins and Mrs Price were summoned to the magistrates' court where they pleaded not guilty to being drunk and disorderly. Witness Special Constable W. Davies backed their plea, informing the bench that in his view the two ladies were sober when brought to the police station. (Davies also conceded that, when they were employed on the munitions, the ladies had lodged with him.) In her evidence Miss Marillier claimed Mrs Price was so inebriated she had fallen. 'I was not drunk,' countered Mrs Price, claiming she slipped because she was experiencing difficulties adjusting to the new studded footwear issued to Land Army women after months in her munitions shoes.

The case was dismissed after the chief constable was called, the exasperated officer reminding the court that his police had no power to detain the women: 'It does not matter how soon you [Miss Marillier] get it out of your head the notion that we can retain them.'

By now the expansion of the munitions works had led to women being lodged across the county from Leominster to Ross. In May more than 200 workers had been welcomed to a tea party at the Royal Hotel in Ross where they also received a rallying talk from Mrs Arnold Foster and Mrs Clowes who, perversely, appealed for more volunteers to join the Women's Land Army. Munitions workers, however, were needed more than ever. That July 134 workers were killed in an explosion at Hereford's sister plant, Chilwell in Nottinghamshire. As a consequence Col Gaudet stepped up production at Rotherwas, introducing a three-shift, 24-hours-a-day working week. Landladies were asked to accommodate the new needs of their shift-working guests while efforts were increased to provide after-work entertainments.

Many munitions workers made their way to the Hereford public library which reported a surge in loans with an average of 228 books being borrowed daily from their stock of 20,000 titles. The city museum also benefited from extra custom and several new donations including some 15th- and 16th-century manuscripts from St Guthlac's Priory and 15 cases of stuffed birds from a Mrs Whiteside. The rules at the welfare club in St Owen Street were changed to allow in women land workers and in July a new outdoor club was started at Edgar Street football ground by Col Gaudet. For a 6d subscription, munitioneers could play tennis and croquet, and, according to the *Hereford Times*, participate in other healthy wholesome sports such as boating, country rambles and gymkhanas.

Swimming was available for 'bathers of both sexes' at the Bartonsham Bathing Station, which had reopened that May after having been closed early due to floods the previous September. The *Hereford Times* reported that 'atmospherical conditions were favourable, the temperature being at summer heat, and the water beautifully clear'. Hereford's Castle Green also remained an important venue for Sunday strollers, although, even as George Lovelock of Park Street was writing to the papers to commend the fine flower displays there, Alderman Wallis was calling on the council to close the park at night because of 'the flapper girls seen to be seducing the men' there.

During the opening of the Edgar Street outdoor club, the Revd Preb Wynne-Wilson had pointed out that, as everyone was going through a difficult time, it was important to keep in good health and remain cheerful. The workers, he said, must go on 'smilingly turning out the material'. Afterwards Lady Butler joined the throng for an evening of dancing and *café chantant* arranged by Harry Rennior with artistes Mr R. Bolton, Mr J. Davies, Mr J. Whalley and Mrs Thornton.

The factory managers, meanwhile, arranged their own entertainments. In January an all-male group of 90 munitions officials, foremen and assistant foremen attended a concert at the Green Dragon Hotel. Col Gaudet presided, asking those present to pause and pay their respects to the late Mr Somerville, who had died recently from pneumonia. Somerville had been moved to Hereford from Morecambe after a disastrous fire

Scandalous goings on in the Castle Green park at night prompted Alderman Wallis to call for the park's closure after dark. This postcard from the time included the following message written on the back in pencil: 'This is where we meet all the Girls at Night after Dark'.

the previous October at the town's White Lund plant, which had killed ten workers. The Green Dragon event was a Smoking Concert, contrast with the fines that continued to be imposed – for the best of reasons given the dire potential consequences – on employees such as James Strangwood, caught with smoking materials at the factory.

A former Stoke Lacy farmworker, Strangwood, who had moved to 2 Millbrook Street, Hereford in July in order to be closer to the factory, was working the new night shift and sending home £2 a week to support his eight brothers and sisters. An old soldier, he had served with the Territorials, been wounded at Gallipoli where he also went down with dysentery and re-enlisted in the Royal Field Artillery at Shoeburyness where he was deafened by a gun blast. He still suffered from dysentery. Caught by factory police with a match in his waistcoat pocket, he explained in court that the offending item would have slipped into his pocket as he handed his contraband (tobacco) to the police on the gate, his persistent dysentery making his hands shake. He was fined £2.

The concerns expressed in 1917 over the behaviour of munitioneers at the Garrick on Sunday nights were dispelled by a report in the local press. On the occasion of the reporter's visit police were said to be guarding the entrances and watching for any unseemly conduct in the long queues for admittance. Inside, the auditorium was packed with factory girls enjoying a programme of music and singing organised by William Batey and the Garrick manager Mr R. Maddox. Communal hymn singing, a picture show entitled *Views of Ceylon* and a performance of *The Vicar of Wakefield* were followed by the Misses Reese of Ross singing songs with illustrations from *The Sunshine of Your Smile*. The new Kinema in St Owen Street, meanwhile, hosted similar entertainments designed, as the observer put it, to 'relieve the tension under which the operatives live and work'.

If their work was tiring, it was also still dangerous. That February coroner Col M.J.G. Scobie opened an inquest into the death of 20-year-old Marie Lotinga from the Black Country. Employed at the filling factory for five months, she had been sent to hospital after feeling unwell and died there on January 25. Scobie listened to evidence from the deputy managing director R.A. Stokes, Medical Officer Dr L.A. Clark and the panel doctor Dr W.B. Butler before concluding that Marie had died from toxic jaundice. Twenty-one-year-old Lily Weaver from Merthyr also died of toxic jaundice. That same month Scobie held an inquest for another factory worker, foreman Albert Hinxman. Having been uprooted from his London home to work at Rotherwas 15 months earlier, he had become depressed and hanged himself at his home in Portland Street.

The tribunals, meanwhile, continued to hear appeals against military service. In April the Hereford Tribunal allowed Alfred Mailes until September and Arthur Williams of the Commercial Hotel until August before they had to enlist, while the case of Hubert Ashmore, a canteen manager at the munitions factory who suffered from gout, was adjourned for medical reports. Tribunal member E.W. Langford withdrew when his fellow members considered the case of Langford's own 41-year-old foreman, cider maker Alfred J. Southall. Langford had described Southall as indispensable to his business and the cider maker was allowed until September. Even then the tribunals were still in session hearing appeals from a 49-year-old Putson market gardener Edward Powles, employed by a Mrs Price; bootmaker Willie Meredith; cycle agent Fred Ladmore; 40-year-old Clifford clog maker and cutter William Beaver; 48-year-old Bromyard gardener and groom George Meredith employed by Mrs Barneby at Brockington; and 44-year-old china dealer, Sam Bibbey from Ross.

The war, however, was drawing to a close. Back in May more than one million US troops had arrived in France signalling defeat for the Germans. The entry of America into the war failed to prevent a local American, William Challis, from being taken to court for omitting to identify himself as a friendly alien. Challis and his wife, a Mordiford woman, lived at the Old Post Office in the village. He had started work at the munitions factory without revealing his US citizenship. 'I hope the Bench will give judgement as though President Wilson was in court,' declared his solicitor, Mr E.L. Wallis, revealing that Challis' son was serving in the British Army. Challis was fined 10 shillings.

The same month, under a banner that promised *No Next Time*, the Ministry of National Service had mounted a recruitment drive for volunteers in Hereford. Almost 1,500 people had crammed into St Peters Square to watch in respectful silence a film, *The Story of Mons*, projected on a huge screen attached to the back of a lorry. It provided recruitment officer Lt C. Teideman with an opportunity to publicly attack those who had refused to fight. 'We have a cure for Pacifists,' he declared. 'We put a rifle in their hands and send them over the top. That is the last we hear of their conscientious objections.' There was laughter from the crowd when he revealed the army nickname for such shirkers. 'We call them skin preservers.'

Such jingoism was not shared by all. That February 22-year-old Lt Geoffrey Bulmer took his Flying Corps service revolver and shot himself. 'Life is such a misery to me now I cannot go on,' he wrote in a suicide note. His death came only days after his parents, Mr and Mrs Percy Bulmer, had attended the funeral of Geoffrey's grandfather, Revd

C.H. Bulmer of Highcroft at Credenhill. The 84-year-old had been rector in the village for almost 50 years.

Credenhill's current rector, Claud Lighton, meanwhile was complaining to the authorities about the treatment of a 19-year-old soldier parishioner, discharged from Pembroke Dock in the late stages of TB and left to walk home to Credenhill from Hereford station. His death a short while later was 'disgraceful negligence', declared Lighton. At Berrington Court that August, family and staff were grieving over the death of Oswald Cawley on the Belgian border. Oswald, who earlier in the year had accepted the nomination to stand as MP for Prestwich following his father's elevation to the House of Lords, was their third son to die.

The Brookes family at Haymeadow Farm in Burghill were also grieving: their lad, Pte Charles Brookes, a former GWR man, had been a POW in Germany. He had drowned while loading coke boats. Around the same time Noah Davies and his wife were astonished when their son Sgt Charles Davies, who had been reported killed two years earlier, suddenly appeared on their doorstep at 7 Mostyn Street, Hereford. Davies had been taken a prisoner of war along with a neighbour from Whitecross, also called Davies. The 22-year-old former Pontrilas postman was said to be the first of the Herefordians to escape from Germany. He would be followed by Alderman Symonds' nephew, Capt William Loder-Symonds who also escaped from a German prisoner of war camp. (Loder-Symonds was destined to die in a flying accident the following May.) British POWs continued to be supported by Louise Luard. She was sending out regular £3 parcels of bread, 'smokes', tea, soup and other items provided by the KSLI prisoners' fund to 34 POWs.

The Germans had begun to release internees and cellist Arthur Evans and vocalist George Ferguson who, along with Hereford Cathedral organist Percy Hull, had been interned at Ruhleben Camp in Berlin for most of the war, were released. Evans and Ferguson returned to Hereford seven months before the end of war, in time to perform at a concert at the Shirehall. Shortly after, news reached the city that Ruhleben prisoner number 177 Civilian Group, Percy Hull, had been freed and was in Scheveningen waiting to board a boat home. Another fortunate Hereford survivor, much to his wife's relief, was Pte Thomas Williams of Church Street. Williams, in civilian life a baker at the India and China Tea Shop, had been returning on board the troopship *Aragon* when it was torpedoed and sunk in the Mediterranean. The destroyer *Attack* was also torpedoed and sank as it circled to pick up survivors. Williams wrote to his wife: 'I think the number missing is well over 1,000.'

There was no let-up in the number of dead and wounded being reported from the front. In April a bomb dropped from an aeroplane had killed L/Cpl Leonard Roberts of the KSLI. The 17-year-old former booking clerk from Leominster station had only recently married Miss Watters from Eardisland. William George Jones from Sellack, who had joined the machine gun corps as a 17-year-old, was killed on the front line.

As another Australian migrant, 27-year-old Pte J. Macklin, a former Credenhill village boy, was killed in France, the Hereford MP, William Hewins, spoke out during a national debate on emigration in parliament. He told the House of Commons that emigration should be left unregulated since it was of the highest importance that British workers and institutions should be available to the Dominions.

Meanwhile Harry and Eliza Male's 20-year-old blacksmith son, Harry, a man who had never worked far from their Woonton home until the outbreak of war, contracted a fever in France and died shoeing army horses. Earlier Col Clowes had been once again defending the continuance of country hunting during a meeting of the North Herefordshire Hunt. Hunt members had gratefully accepted an offer from Major Heygate to carry on as master in the coming season on a gratuity of £600 as Clowes pointed out that the cavalry would not be mounted, but for the hunts. 'Many of the soldiers in France today proved all the better soldiers through having ridden straight to hounds in England,' he declared. His only son, 20-year-old Warren 'Pat' Clowes, had been killed in France days earlier. Mr and Mrs J.E. Ellis of Lower Court, Bridge Street, Leominster were grieving over the death of their 19-year-old son, Pte Leonard Ellis, their fourth son to have died in the war, while the Lucas-Tooth's third son, Archibald died in July.

The death of Col Clive in France earlier in April prompted an unseemly wrangle over his successor as MP for South Herefordshire. The Farmers' Union put up their own man, Alderman Thomas Preece, against the favoured Unionist Association candidate, Charles Pulley, while Col Clive's wife Muriel wrote to the press: 'I have given my all but were my two sons of fighting age they would by now be filling their father's place in the thin battle line. I beg of the men to go to the Front and to trust us women to carry on.'

As a woman she was still not entitled to vote in the resulting by-election, which took place in May and which saw a straight fight between Pulley and Thomas Preece. The press judged it a quiet election, neither candidate displaying flamboyant party colours or being able to tour the polling stations because of fuel rationing. With so many men at war, Pulley polled 3,260 votes out of the 11,000 electors to Preece's 1,784. One letter writer, D.A. Griffiths of Peterchurch, was pleased with the result, reporting that the corncrake or landrail had commenced calling in the Golden Valley 'as if in celebration of Mr Pulley's triumph'.

Colonel Clowes (right) of Burton Court continued to defend hunting, which continued through the war. 'Many proved all the better soldiers through having ridden straight to hounds,' he declared only days after his 20-year-old son Pat was killed in France. (Photo: Eardisland Heritage & History Group)

The lack of voting rights for women climbed the local agenda. Earlier in the year the issue was debated at the Garrick Theatre with Mrs Dymond, Mrs Baker, a former brick-layer and chairman of the Trades Council George Davies and the Labour leader Sidney Box, secretary of the Herefordshire Labour Representational Committee. Women, Box declared, could not make a bigger muddle in national and international affairs than men had done. The muddle was set to continue.

When C.W. Gertner of 55 Green Street was appointed, briefly, to the post of wood-carving master at the Art School in July, Alderman James Corner protested to his fellow members on the Education Committee: 'We want no Germans there.' When it was pointed out that Gertner was born in England of German parentage, Corner remained unimpressed: 'He may have been born in England but that does not change the fact that he is German by blood, one of the most brutal of all the human races.' The matter was dropped when the committee learned that Gertner had stepped down and was now before the city tribunal. But the artist concerned was deeply upset by the slur on his name. Revealing that he had been born in Wales and that his father was Portuguese not German, Gertner explained that he had lived in the city for 18 years and had a brother serving on machine guns somewhere in France. 'I am suffering a great misfortune in having a foreign name,' he told the newspapers.

There was also confusion over new rules on 'treating', the business of buying drinks for friends, which had been outlawed under the Defence of the Realm Act in an effort to reduce drunkenness. Several generous drinkers were brought to court charged with breaking the treating law after police in plain clothes raided the Market Tavern, The Barrels in Eign Street and Number 10 in Widemarsh Street. Fines ranging from £1 to £10 were handed down. George Crump from the Camp Inn and William George from the Travellers Rest at Stretton were also fined for allowing out of hours drinking while the 70 licensees in Ross were singled out by the licensing authorities for their lax attitude towards the treating orders.

The cathedral's 80-year-old dean, meanwhile, was still battling intemperance. His alcohol-free Dean Leigh coffee canteen had been formally opened at the Market. It was, he said, a good piece of temperance work: 'These men drove animals many miles in all sorts of weather and ought to earn the gratitude, not only of the farmers but the public in general.'

The public exhibited their generosity in a variety of ways. Sarnesfield VAD Hospital, for example, became the unexpected beneficiary of a lawsuit after blacksmith Thomas Llewellyn accused six Dilwyn men of libelling him in a letter. The men had sent a written complaint to the local military representative, Sir Geoffrey Cornewall, following a row between Llewellyn and a somewhat imperious local doctor. The Hereford assizes judge found in Llewellyn's favour and awarded the blacksmith £6 damages which Llewellyn promptly presented to the hospital.

A more substantial gift of £1,000 from Abergavenny surveyor Frank Mansfield allowed the Hereford Hospital board to buy Wolseley Villa in Mill Street to accommodate more nurses: all nursing leave had been cancelled in August as the hospital struggled to cope with a sudden influx of 180 wounded soldiers. It marked the arrival of the Herefordshire Regiment in France. The *Hereford Times* revealed: 'The veil of secrecy of [the Regiment's] whereabouts was lifted on Monday with dramatic suddenness when the wounded young warriors arrived in Hereford.' The Regiment, engaged in the Second Battle of the Marne, had suffered severe casualties including eight officers and 230 other ranks in a single day. Wounds ranged from shell shock to amputation and amongst those wounded were Lt Howard Bulmer from Longmeadow, Colour Sgt Maj Young from Ross, Pte R.C. Evans, who had been gassed, from Sellack Marsh, L/Cpl W.R. Gurney from the White Hart in Ledbury and 39-year-old H.A. Lamputt from 81 Bath Street.

There were now sufficient wounded service men in the county for the National Federation of Discharged Soldiers, Sailors and War Pensioners to open a district office at 11 Gomond Street, chaired by Mr Morris of Shucknall. The Federation, which claimed to have prevented at least one service widow from being evicted from her home (was this Leominster's Annie Strangwood?), advocated seizing unclaimed German bank balances in the country and spending the money on wounded servicemen.

At Bromyard the Boys Own Brotherhood demonstrated their generosity by holding a fundraising Sunday Soldiers' Photograph Day, displaying family member pictures (they had only recently attended a memorial service for 25-year-old Pte William Rose, killed in action in France) while at Orcop school, children collected enough money to buy a wristwatch which was presented to their former headmaster, now Signaller John Davies, when he arrived home on leave.

Herefordians proved less generous than their neighbours in Ross during that July's War Weapons Week. The city aimed to raise around £50,000 for a Hereford named war weapon, but by mid-July it was still short of £34,000. Ross managed to find £50,000 during its own Aeroplane Week, the fundraising stimulated by the unexpected arrival of a Royal Flying Corps Sopwith Camel which made an emergency landing at Hildersley after running out of fuel. It was flown out two days later, the pilot performing an Immelmann turn, a strategic but dangerous manoeuvre developed by fighter pilots, over the town.

At Bodenham Mr J. Simpson mounted a charity lecture tour that earned over £100 for the St Dunstan Hostel for Blinded Soldiers while Lady Cotterell's shilling draw raised £2,500 for the Red Cross. Its funds had already been boosted by a painting presented to the city by Col Clive before his death. It depicted the 1st Battalion Herefordshire Regiment's Suvla landings, a realistic likeness according to Sgt C. Bracher. Copies of the painting were offered at 2 shillings each, the money being donated to the Red Cross, an organisation which was busier than it had ever been. During the final three months of 1917 the Red Cross raised £3,000, spending £2,500 on hospitals, ambulances and equipment for Hampton Grange. The funds also helped nuns from the Sisters of Charity of St Vincent de Paul who had left their monastery at Lower Bullingham to work with the Red Cross in France.

As Mr A. Pudsey Dawson of Ryeland Street arranged collections of fresh eggs to be sent to the front, local women continued to help out at the Barrs Court Rest Station, a facility that had fed no less than 41,000 soldiers during 1917.

Food was on everyone's mind. In June the Food Control Committee, in response to the government's introduction of rationing, dispatched 51,000 new ration books. (The Hereford Motor Company did a brisk trade with its special ration card holders, price 1s 3d, for meat, sugar and butter.) As the fats ration for butter and margarine was raised from 4 ounces to 5 ounces, the committee ordered citizens to take two-thirds of their summer meat rations in frozen form to conserve supplies of fresh meat.

The committee also processed all applications for precious supplies of preserving sugar. Leominster had its own Food Control Committee. It refused a request from the town's milk retailers for a 1d increase on a gallon of milk (they had been charging 3d a pint or 1s 10d a gallon although, by June, the price of a quart had risen by a penny to 6d), while in Hereford the mayor opened a National Kitchen at the Market Hall. Serving economical and nourishing cooked lunches, the kitchen's running costs were met by the Corporation, although it was run on strict business terms.

Bromyard was promised a new cheese factory by the county council while the new co-operative cheese factory at Dinmore celebrated its success in acquiring its first 60 cheese customers. The cheese was made from 800 gallons of milk delivered weekly by train from as far away as Ludlow, Risbury and Hereford. The factory's celebratory tea was laid on by the Jones family from Wellington Court.

All this effort was not enough to prevent food queues winding down the streets, leaving one shopper complaining that 'we never see the well-to-do lined up'. Another, with three children under 16, wrote to the *Hereford Times*: 'Now that my husband being 46 must either join up or do farm work, I would like to know how we are to manage on 31 shillings a week.'

The humble hen had become a valuable commodity. Mesira Hoskins and his wife Valentine from Sutton's Marsh were taken to court for stealing four fowl at Preston Wynne. Even the benign clergyman Cornish Watkins, a keen naturalist who noted with sadness the shooting of a rare bittern in the rushy ground at Titley the previous Christmas Eve, watched with hungry regret as a flock of wild geese flew over 'within easy gunshot, given the present scarcity of food and the price of geese at the Christmas markets'.

Pig clubs began to emerge (one had started up at Holmer that June) where householders clubbed together to feed a pig and share the meat when it was killed. Henry Wadworth of Breinton Court pointed out that the food being wasted on the nation's estimated 5 million dogs could be put to better use by raising a million pigs. Wadworth was especially vexed by dog owners, his ewes having recently been attacked by a pair of Sealyham terriers. At Kington, however, John and Margaret Edwards were heavily fined for lavishing too much care on their pigs. They were caught fattening the beasts on quality whole wheat and barley flour, which was only to be used for breadmaking.

One solution to the problem was to produce more food on the city's 500 allotments, especially given the findings of Mr R. Bird, who wrote to the local press revealing his highly productive yields resulting from his applying a small electrical charge to growing crops. That summer saw 100 people on the city waiting list for allotments as plans were revealed for an additional 300 allotments to be provided in Belmont Road, Whitehorse Street, Edgar Street, Rockfield Road and Portfield Street.

A campaign to allow the netting of river fish for public consumption was still rumbling along. It received a boost when Mr J. Arthur Hutton of Colcombe, Hampton Bishop revealed that fish stocks were on the increase. He reported that the rod catch for salmon had amounted to 2,384 fish averaging 16.5lbs. (One 80-year-old fisherman, G.W. Carlyon landed a fish well above average: a salmon at Ross that weighed in at 46.5lbs.) The reluctant Wye Board of Conservators was eventually persuaded to allow the netting of fish for public consumption, but the plans never ran smoothly. The first fish were to be sold at 2 shillings per pound weight to the poor, considerably below the controlled price as the Conservators pointed out. Arthur Hutton himself contributed ten salmon to the scheme while complaining about high levels of pollution near the Hereford sewage works which threatened the health of the fish and, presumably, those who consumed them.

Almost 300 householders hoping to enjoy a little fresh salmon were instructed to apply, in writing, that June to the Food Control's National Kitchen supervisor in the market. In the event between 500 and 600lbs of salmon and one hundredweight of coarse fish were sold on the day. But T.J. Stokes from Hay insisted that the Conservators were not playing fair over the sale of fish. His parish had been informed that there were no fish available and yet he had witnessed the sale of a netted salmon on the riverbank. 'So the cupboard was bare for the people of Hay who were expecting to get a bit of luxury for once in their lives,' he declared.

By late summer, fruit collection schemes ('maximum government prices paid') were served by several receiving stations including the vicarage at Brinsop, the Green Man club room in Fownhope and Castle End at Lea. Even nutshells and fruit stones, used to make charcoal for gas masks by the Ministry of Munitions, were being collected by the sackful.

After the government's food production department had warned that the 1918 potato crop would prove even more vital than the previous year's, countywide lectures on potato growing were laid on. Meanwhile the Hereford Girls' College announced plans to start beekeeping courses as county beekeepers, still badly affected by the spread of disease in their hives, began distributing fresh nuclei at the subsidised cost of 10 shillings each.

Relations between food producers and local inspectors, never good at the best of times, were worsening. When a spot check was carried out in Ledbury on the milk from Thomas Theyer's Swords Farm at Liddington, he tipped the entire contents of the churn into the road. 'There', he told the inspector in a fit of pique. 'Take a sample of that! I won't bring another ****** drop of milk to Ledbury.' He was hauled before the magistrates and fined £25. Earlier that year Thomas Davies, a conscientious objector who farmed at Little Dewchurch, steadfastly refused to make a return on his livestock to inspectors on the grounds that it would be mocking the Lord to do so. He was fined £5 for his troubles. Tenbury baker John Wormington was caught and fined for selling good bread to German POWs at Lindridge, and Hereford butcher Herbert Cresswell landed himself in trouble when he sold veal in contravention of rationing. He was fined £20.

Fuel prices rose as the year wore on. The spiralling price of coal had already forced the city authorities to raise the 30 shillings a day hire cost of its steam roller. In May munitions worker Albert Percy Chadney of Whitehorse Street, Hereford had been fined £1 for the misuse of petrol after being caught driving his motorcycle through Ledbury. The Drybridge House doctor, G.H.H. Symonds, was similarly charged with the misuse of petrol when PC Greenway noticed the medic's car parked in a field at Aconbury with two dead rabbits and a spade in the back. The magistrates dismissed the case of wasting fuel when the doctor explained that he had stopped to do some ferreting having visited a patient at Aconbury.

Another local doctor, Paul Chapman, was summoned for using petrol in his motor-cycle and sidecar at Cascob. He explained that he kept a bungalow at Cascob and after working as the physician at Beechwood and Sarnesfield and conducting surgeries on Saturdays, often until 8pm, he was in dire need of some recreation for his own health. The magistrates sympathised but were obliged to hand out a fine of 10 shillings.

Fuel shortages hit the household as well as the motorist and Hereford's munic-ipal electricity costs more than doubled from £12,000 to £27,000. By August the fuel shortage was so critical that when a rick fire broke out on tenant farmer Mr N. Bayliss' farm at Ullingswick, he had to send three of his own horses to collect the Nell Gwynne fire engine from Hereford. Earlier in the year Mayor Dymond had appealed for more volunteer firemen following a motor car fire in High Town which scorched the cab rank. Now, as the county entered the peak season for rick fires, Councillor Ridler called for a motor fire engine to be based in the district. It was ironic that, with an explosives factory so close to the city, the fire service was still managing with a horse-drawn engine.

The Hereford fire service before the war. The service was still managing with horse-drawn equipment when a rick fire at Ullingswick compelled farmer Bayliss to send his own horses to fetch the engine. (Postcard: Derrick Blake)

The relentless and depressing austerity proved too much for some: rail travellers at Ross Station were shocked when the manager of the Swan Hotel, 49-year-old Miss Evelyn Read, stepped down from the platform and calmly lay down in front of the Hereford train. She was killed instantly.

The economic conditions put a strain on industrial relations and in September 500 of the city's 600 railway workers went on strike for four days in pursuit of a national increase of 10 shillings a week. Union leaders blamed 'the exorbitant increase in the cost of commodities'. By then a first-class driver with 38 years' service was paid between £3 13s and £4 3s a week with a war bonus of 25 shillings. Porters earned £2 5s exclusive of tips, compared with £1 a week before the war. (Coal miners were earning up to £15 a week, according to the railway workers.) The strike earned the railway workers few friends. According to the authorities the 'movement of munitions of war was severely disrupted' while munitions workers, deprived of their means of transport to the factory, were said to be disgusted at the decision which affected their efforts to, as one put it, 'keep the boys at the front up'.

Their work, however, was soon to come to an abrupt end. Many could see it coming although factory numbers peaked at 3,982 women and 1,882 men that October. In her July 1918 report, Lilian Barker had given a breakdown of where the workers were employed: nearly 4,000 worked on filling, 673 in stores and engineering. (There were more people employed on policing the factory – 135 – than in the offices or canteens.) The munitioneers were among the first to learn officially that the war was over. Col Gaudet called them together: 'It is just two years ago today that the first shell was filled in the factory, and since then millions of tons of explosives have been turned out for the destruction of the Huns.' National Filling Factory 14 had, he said, been one of the great munitions works of England and he paid tribute to the workers who were given the rest of the day off. The girls responded with impromptu performances of *Rule Britannia* and *La Marseillaise* before heading into the city to celebrate.

The factory closed at the end of November and the estimated weekly wages bill of over £15,000 came to an end as the last 500 workers left. Most of the Lancashire cotton mill workers were said to have already left of their own accord. There were muted celebrations and parties: at Ross the Munitions Girls' Club held a fancy dress ball at the Corn Exchange and presented Mr A.W. Ursell with a smoker's cabinet, and munitioneer Mrs Lucy Foster with a brass inkstand.

But there had been a perceptible sense that the war was coming to an end from the start of 1918, one anonymous clergyman warning in a letter to the *Hereford Times* 'when peace comes … millions of men and women will be demobilised'. That summer Albert Simpson of Burghill Grange recommended that after the war nothing should be purchased which was of German origin. 'Our Government, purged as I hope it will be of German influence, will aid our producers by placing a heavy tariff on all German productions.'

Hereford's city fathers, meanwhile, were planning to build between 10,000 and 15,000 new homes on 2,250 acres. The county council opposed the plans, fearful that the city expected to expand beyond its boundaries into the surrounding rural districts. The county council's objections would leave the poor 'playing in the streets,' claimed Alderman Bulmer (also a city councillor). 'Well, your interests lie there,' scolded Councillor James Corner. The Institute of Sanitary Engineers, however, was fully behind the plans. At their conference in May, and after their meatless meal at the Green Dragon and a visit to the city sewage works (much admired for its efficient system which included the growing of withies that were made, on the premises, into the corporation's fruit baskets), members turned to discuss housing. County surveyor G.H. Jack condemned the 'mostly inconvenient and insanitary conditions' that pertained in the majority of Herefordshire's picturesque country cottages. Members discussed how the homes of working people should be designed in future (no more chilly parlours or tin baths hanging in sculleries), while Herbert Skyrme called for more use to be made of damp-proof coursing and concrete block work.

The sanitary engineers also congratulated Hereford city planners for pulling down the slums around St Owen Street. Slum housing and the wartime absences of fighting men and working women were seen as being partly responsible for the rising problem of juvenile delinquency. In June, 14-year-old Thomas Jay, James Richardson, aged 12, and James Scott, also aged 12, all of Catherine Street, Hereford were bound over after stealing three bottles of Indian Pale Ale from the Great Western Railway. Sixteen-year-old Charles Preece was hauled before magistrates for stealing apples growing at Portfields (the case was adjourned to allow Preece to find a job), and George Smart of Burcott Road was fined 5 shillings with 10 shillings damages for uprooting 17 precious rows of potatoes. (His father complained that every time he tried to chastise the boy, his neighbours complained.)

In a bid to tackle this social problem, plans were unveiled to open a play centre at Scudamore School. There would be further meetings between organisations such as the YMCA, Girls' Friendly Society and the Ministry of Munitions over city play centres amidst continued complaints about gangs of lads, their fathers away on active service, roaming free in the Widemarsh Street area. The situation got out of hand when 81-year-old James Shewring took fright and fired a gun directly at a group of boys, injuring 14-year-old William Jones and 15-year-old Fred Matthews, who was shot in the face.

Young people were not alone in breaking the law. Pixley postmistress Mabel Faulkner had been sent to prison for three months after stealing £71 from the post office, while a 17-year-old Much Birch postman, William Prosser, was fined £5 when he was found to have thrown away 36 postal packages on his round. The postman, who was earning 21s 6d a week, told Harewood End police court he was tired of walking the round. In London meanwhile, Sir Richard Rankin was brought before Marylebone magistrates after carousing with three street musicians at his London lodgings, Cox's Hotel in Jermyn Street. He was fined £20 for what police described as 'a discreditable and scandalous case'.

Chauffeur Richard Ravenhill was acquitted of dangerous driving after knocking down and killing factory worker Mrs Emma Morris in Belmont Road, Hereford. He told the court that he had driven over 150,000 miles for his employer Mr Stephen Beeson.

Such incidents were on the increase. That summer the police were called when a Ministry of Munitions car driven by Pte Ernest Rizoul crashed into a Food Prosecution motor car driven by Pte F.G. Robinson in St Martin's Street. No action was taken after Rizoul explained that he had swerved to avoid a dog. And no action was taken against a government tractor supervisor who collided with, and killed, 6-year-old Arthur Morris while he was playing in the road at Yazor. After hearing that the motorcyclist, W.D. Jones, had sounded his horn and later made a gift of £5 towards the funeral expenses of the farm labourer's son, the coroner at the child's inquest attached no blame to him.

By then a far bigger spectre loomed on the horizon. In July a severe storm hit the county, lightning striking an outhouse at the Three Horseshoes in Kingsland, bursting a barrel of cider and burning the buttons on the tunic of PC Roland Preece, on duty at Cobnash. Mr Challoner at the Bridge Inn, Michaelchurch Escley, lost three ewes and a lamb, struck by lightning. The storm presaged a new threat, according to the local press: an epidemic of influenza. The cathedral choral services were cancelled as a safety measure. The city's Board of Guardians closed the workhouse to visitors (it was reopened for the bishop's thanksgiving service there in September), and when 59-year-old acting constable Francis Smith of Grenfell Road became depressed that August and killed himself by cutting his throat, his son blamed his father's depression on a bout of influenza.

In July mourners gathered for the full military funeral of Pte Cyril Hewart Moore, a 21-year-old whose parents ran Leominster's Bird in Hand public house. Cyril had only recently married the daughter of the landlord at Hereford's Lichfield Vaults, Nellie Vaughan. Cyril had succumbed to influenza and died at Beechwood hospital. Spanish flu, as it became known, claimed the lives Capt J.F. Leather, the son of Ella Mary Leather and Lt Col Francis H. Leather, and former Henry Weston cider worker, Pte C.H. Hall of Newton Villas, Ashfield Road, Ross. The pandemic, its spread hastened by the movement of troops, was to kill many more mostly young, healthy men.

RAMC ambulance man Robert Bellamy headed home at the end of the war to the family farm at Penallt. 'Old Pritchard was at The Lion [inn] then and I think they had a sort of a celebration supper. I couldn't go because I had this awful Spanish flu.

'We were coming back from Egypt and when we reached the south of Italy, Brindisi, it was terribly cold. We were absolutely perished, you know? And we were put in trucks to come up to Le Havre, right up through the Alps. We were about forty in a truck, with all our kit, rifles and some of the fellows were terribly ill. Some died on the way up.'

Arthur reached Southampton and was put on a train back to his home station at Fawley. Word of his arrival had reached the family: 'My sister met me, and the old man [his father] was there as well, but he got on the train and went off to Ross market! He hadn't seen me for about two years.'

Arthur's sister helped him home. 'I went down to Fawley Court in the evening to see them down there, and they thought I was a ghost.' Then Arthur took to his bed for a month. He nearly died. Later in life he would reflect on the war and the carnage it caused in his home village: 'Revd Whitehouse, his son was killed. And the two Cartwright brothers who lived in the cottage opposite the farm. There was a Brewer, I think and a Clarke. There was Humphrey Brandon-Jones's brother Richard, he won the VC. But you see, it wasn't like it is now: there wasn't the attention then. You just died. And that was it.'

Chapter 7

1919

Bromyard had marked the armistice by forcing Union Jacks on its German POWs and burning an effigy of Kaiser Wilhelm II. In Ledbury too the Kaiser was burned while Leominster's citizens gathered in Corn Square to sing hymns and weep. The time had come to recover from war. For women over 30 it was time to vote.

The 1918 Representation of the People Act gave the vote to all men over 21 and all women over 30. Despite his reputation as a moderniser, the Bishop of Hereford had 'the deepest misgivings' over this change to the electoral register. At a meeting to discuss the issue, chaired by Mayor Dymond shortly before the general election, the bishop expressed his concerns over women's political inexperience. He was also worried that they might choose to organise themselves politically 'as a sex'. He need not have worried.

The countywide election results contained few surprises, both the Conservative candidates being elected, Charles Pulley to William Hewins' seat (which had been extended to take in the former South Hereford seat) and Major Charles Ward-Jackson for Leominster. However it was clear that women voters had been out in force. According to Ward-Jackson they included a 90-year-old lady from Bishops Frome who had expressed the hope that this would not be her last election. The turnout in the Hereford and South Herefordshire constituency had exceeded 50%, the number of eligible voters having almost trebled from 11,000 to 28,246 thanks to the extra voters.

Having won the previous by-election, Charles Pulley was opposed by the farm leader, Sidney Box, in a class battle that would have been inconceivable in 1914. Box, with his constant attacks on the establishment, had risen in prominence through the war. In October 1918 he was elected to the HWAC executive. Later he would be invited to join the Agricultural Wages Board. His profile, published by the local press on the eve of the election, revealed that he had been born at Mathon near the Malverns in 1873, one of 17 children. Orphaned at eight, he had become a child labourer by the age of nine, working on farms. A self-educated Victorian, the small, dapper 45-year-old was now president of the Trades Council and a determined opponent to pedigree Hereford breeder and former banker 54-year-old Charles Pulley, the squire of Eaton Bishop. Box was never going to win but in the event he was gratified to receive 3,730 votes to Pulley's 11,680.

The turnout by voters in the Leominster constituency was even higher than in Hereford. Here the three-way battle between the Conservative Ward-Jackson, the former Liberal MP now standing as an Independent Edmund Lamb, and the farmers' man, E.W. Langford attracted a 63% turnout and a majority of just over 3,000 for the Tory candidate who headed off to Parliament.

Langford was rueful about coming third, but for now his farming colleagues had a more pressing matter to contend with: the tardy release of agricultural men from the services. As soon as the armistice was declared, HWAC had sent a request to the military authorities for the return of 180 key agricultural men. In the event only one had been returned and a letter asking for procedures to be speeded up was dispatched to the Board of Agriculture. Alderman Bulmer, who stressed that obtaining the men was 'of supreme and urgent importance', conjectured that older men were being kept in the camps because overpaid colonels on large pay were hanging on to their soldiers for as long as possible to keep the regiments at full strength.

The stress of being kept in camp proved too much for one former Hereford soldier, 58-year-old Sgt Michael Sullivan, cooped up in the barracks at Newport. Overcome with fury and frustration he strode into a hut where his senior sergeant was playing cards and shot him dead. 'And if the sergeant major was there I would have killed him too,' the unrepentant Sullivan told police.

Until they received their men back, the farmers had to make do with POWs and women. In the south of the county, one gang of prisoners of war had been travelling from farm to farm to help out. Local farmers were gratified to learn that a POW camp at Llandinabo was to become a base for 40 prisoners. In the Dore district 50 German POWs billeted at the local workhouse were already assisting with the mending of the parish roads.

As for the Land Army girls, just over 2,500 women had been registered in 186 different parishes for farm work during the course of the war, according to the HWWAC. Now however, the organisation reported a fall in numbers with no more than 243 working on the county's farms. The committee's Miss Maddison said that some girls were already asking to be demobilised: since they had signed up for a year and had not yet completed their time, their requests had been refused. But as 41 of her land girls picked up their good service badges at the Town Hall that February (afterwards they slipped out for a free meal at the National Kitchen), Miss Maddison reported that several girls were training near Ross at Great Howle Farm under a Mrs Harris, 4 girls were on thatching and a further 20 had 'pulled roots' for 15 different farmers. Seven newly trained women were available for milking and horse work and one for ploughing. There was, she added, no trouble over pay, farmers often agreeing to pay over the minimum fixed wage of 22s 6d rising to 25s a week.

Many farms still gave cider as part of the wage. Towards the end of 1918 temperance supporters including Revd H.L. Somers Cocks from Eastnor and Revd T. Holland from Little Marcle had met with the South Herefordshire farmers to try and dissuade them from continuing this practice. 'We should be only too pleased if this cider habit could be abolished,' conceded Harewood End farmer Mr P. Preece, being careful not to make any firm commitment. The farm workers' leader Sidney Box was appalled by the outmoded business of paying for work with drink: 'No other workers would put up with

Many farmers still offered cider as part of the wages, a practice condemned by labour rights campaigner Sidney Box as 'unfair and unjust'.
(Photo: Winnie Reece)

such unfair and unjust payment,' he said, adding the curious warning: 'The labourers and the [Workers'] Union have shown patriotism by refraining from pressing their just claims during the war. After the war, wait and see.'

Farmers also had to contend with the unpopular cultivation orders requiring them to plough fresh land. Towards the end of 1918, Longtown farmers had held a protest meeting at the New Inn to voice their objections to cultivation orders on the grounds that much of their land was too 'banky' for the plough. Many orders remained in place that spring and over 240 farms were still classed as 'under observation'. The restrictions, however, were expected to be lifted soon and HWAC agreed to continue hiring out tractor ploughs while selling off any surplus machines. (In April HWAC revealed that a total of 34,000 Herefordshire acres had been put to the plough during the war, compared to the final target of 37,000 acres of virgin sward.)

There was good news from the government's experimental station on Kings Acre Road, which reported significantly improved yields from the use of an overhead electrical system.

While the farmers looked for labourers, returning soldiers looked for land. The promise of homes for heroes embraced a national campaign to find smallholdings for returning soldiers who might receive some compensation for their front line traumas. More than 100 soldiers had applied to Herefordshire County Council for a smallholding, the land area required representing around 4,300 acres. Many in the farming community were bemused by the idea: where was the land to be had? How would the scheme impact on the county's traditional agricultural economy? And what did soldiers know about farming?

The Board of Agriculture announced it would offer farmers 30 shillings a week to retrain former army officers in agriculture while the county council set up a smallholdings sub-committee to consider the matter, Councillor Bulmer advocating that the committee co-opt representatives from the working classes. Land agent W.J. Davies was appointed to look at the land question as several councillors wondered if the now redundant factory land at Rotherwas or Credenhill could be utilised for the servicemen. It could not: that April, in answer to a parliamentary question from Charles Pulley, the Ministry of Munitions announced that Rotherwas was now being used to dismantle munitions. It was meeting a weekly wages bill of £10,339 with 99 people (52 men and 47 women) at the former filling factory and 923 (550 men and 373 women) employed to recover steel, brass, lead and resin from munitions. The minister, Winston Churchill, also announced that the government intended to keep hold of its storage facility at Credenhill.

Several county councillors, many of them significant landowners in their own right, advocated a cautionary approach to the popular, if, they thought, ill-conceived idea of giving small farms to servicemen. During their deliberations in February, Cpt Hinckes suggested that the applicants might be better served taking up employment on the land, while Councillor Russell offered what, to many grieving families, was a particularly insensitive observation – that landlords 'had not had a rosy time during the last three or four years'. Reminding members that while tithes had risen and repairs cost three times as much as before the war, rents had not been raised unless a farm changed hands, he went on: 'If any class had suffered it was that consisting of the landlords.'

Meanwhile, after the celebratory excesses of November's post-war parties, people cast about for any diversions free from the taint of war. Alfred Watkins advocated the radical notion of changing the coin of the realm to an octaval system. The idea was less well received than one from the Board of Agriculture proposing a new, 104 mile, narrow gauge rail network for Herefordshire.

Thousands of miles of narrow gauge railways in France, used to ferry troops and munitions to the front, were to be dismantled. The British Government indicated that, as a national experiment, it was prepared to recover some of the rail and rolling stock and reinstall it as an electrically powered light railway centred on Hereford Market. The rail would extend to Llangarron, Woolhope, Bromyard, Bredwardine, Lingen and Leintwardine and there was talk of a government grant amounting to £2,000 per mile. Such a railway, said its advocates, had the potential to increase productivity, raise the social conditions of people in rural areas and improve the poor quality of its housing stock. (As Britain headed towards a national housing crisis Hereford's district council had identified a local need for 224 new 'cottages'. But they were expensive to build at £400 a unit – it represented a rent of 2/6d a week – and councillors, mindful of the coming May elections, put discussions on hold. Their temerity caused Revd R.G. Morgan, the rector at Stoke Lacy, to publicly attack landlords for the state of Herefordshire's country working homes, which he claimed were mostly unfit to live in.)

'If the war has taught us one thing, it has taught us to appreciate the agricultural industry as a national asset,' said one a Board of Agriculture spokesman as the railway plan was put before the HWAC. And the more the idea was discussed, the more support it gathered. By February, Leominster, Ledbury, Ross, Weobley and New Radnor had all declared in its favour. As Alderman Bulmer put it: 'If you want people to live on the land you must take the railways to them.'

Some had their reservations. John Johnson, writing to the press from Bryngwyn Cottages, conceded the railway would be ideal for taking 'ripe timber' from distant parts, but believed the immediate area of ten miles around Hereford was better served by roads. (The nation's woodlands had been seriously plundered of its timber stocks and a forestry commission was set up in 1919 charged with reforesting Britain.) Kington's Mr J. Edwards, meanwhile, was minded to ask whether the old Titley to Eardisley railway, removed to France for the movement of troops at the outset of war, was to be returned. He was assured it was.

Many, however, were too preoccupied by grief to give a thought to railways or woodlands. Shortly before Christmas Mrs Candy of Almeley, whose husband was still in the forces, succumbed to influenza and died, leaving eight children including a 17-month-old blind boy. The influenza outbreak, which saw all schools in Herefordshire temporarily closed in early 1919, also claimed the life of the aviator who had first flown over Hereford's Bartonsham Meadows in 1913, test pilot Bentfield Hucks.

Londoner Annie Button with her children after her husband had been taken prisoner of war. Moved to the Hereford munition works, she returned home when her husband was repatriated. He died of tuberculosis in December. A week later her son, little Billy, also died. (Photo: Sara Tait)

Most of the munitioneers had gone home, dismissed from service on 11 November 1918 by Col Gaudet who had returned to Canada to take charge of the Montreal police and fire forces. Some of the Rotherwas workers stayed on, including Nellie Lambert. 'When the war ended only five workers were kept on for cleaning. I was kept on because my father had died in the services,' she remembered years later. She was soon joined by other workers: 'Men out of the services were sent to the factory to break down the ammunition and it was there I met my husband-to-be.' Nellie Lambert became Nellie Williams.

When a photograph of Nellie and a group of fellow workers in their munitions uniform was published in a national magazine almost a century after the factory had closed, a reader in another part of the country was surprised to recognise her own grandmother, Annie Button, amongst the group. 'I knew she had done war work,' wrote Annie's granddaughter, Sara Tait, 'but I couldn't understand how this woman with three children under the age of 6 and living in the heart of London at King's Cross could have been in Hereford.' It transpired that Annie's husband Bill had enlisted in the Kings Royal Rifle Corps in 1914 and been captured the same year by the Germans. Annie, leaving her children with friends or relatives, had joined the munitions, probably at Woolwich, and been moved to Rotherwas. When the factory closed, and as her husband was repatriated, Annie returned to London. A week later on 17 December Bill Button died of tuberculosis. Their little boy Billy died seven days later.

As MPs joined the new coalition government on their member's wage of £400 a year, women such as Annie started to receive their war widow's pensions: 13s 9d per week for the wife of a private, rising to 21s 3d for a senior soldier. The pension was paid to common-law wives and married women alike, but women had to forgo their widow's pension if, as Annie did, they remarried. (Although she remarried and raised a new family, Annie harboured a deep hatred for the German people for the rest of her life.)

By now the footballing girls, Sadie and Honor Lloyd and friends Beatrice and Dolly Taylor were finding husbands of their own. Dolly had married in 1918, Honor married one of the factory sentries and Sadie, in 1920, married Cyril, Beatrice's and Dolly's brother, a year before the Football

The munition workers Dolly and Beatrice Taylor were stood down when the munition factory closed. Neither enjoyed good health after working there, Beatrice dying shortly after the Armistice and Dorothy in 1926. (Photo: Tim Smith)

Association banned women's football from its grounds for the next 50 years. (The munitions men had played their final match at the end of 1918 with a match between the Factory and the 'Agriculturalists'.) Neither Beatrice nor Dolly enjoyed good health after working at the factory: Beatrice died shortly after armistice and Dorothy died in 1926. They were to share the same grave.

Their illnesses may have been associated with exposure to dangerous chemicals at the factory. Although it would not emerge until many years later, the poisons handled at Rotherwas included mustard gas. John Edmonds in his book *The History of Rotherwas Munitions Factory, Hereford* revealed that shells were being charged with mustard gas at Rotherwas from 11 October 1918 and that by the end of the war almost 4,000 mustard gas shells had been filled there.

Yet according to the local press the 'first fatality at the factory' involved 19-year-old Winifred Aulsebrook, killed as she dismantled munitions in 1920. The explosion in April 1920 also injured Annie Tranter: the two women had been counting fuses.

Winnie's brother Harry, who had married another munitioneer, Elsie Moss, was called to identify his sister's body.

Anxious parents like Peterchurch stonemason Alfred Verrill and his wife Hannah were relieved to have their munitioneer daughter Kitty safely home, but the waiting was not yet over. They had heard that their eldest son, named Alfred after his father, was on his way home from Egypt – as a gardener at How Caple Alfred had joined his employer's regiment – but there was no word from George, their 20-year-old son. During the war the main channels of communication over missing men on either side had been the Red Cross. Their workers checked hospital admissions, interviewed wounded soldiers for news of missing comrades and passed on the names of missing men given to their staff in Geneva by both sides. But information from Germany slowed down as the war went in favour of the Allies and Hannah wrote letter after letter to the authorities appealing for news of George. It was not until several years later that his possessions were finally returned and she was told: 'We are very sorry to report your son was taken prisoner of war.' He had died in October 1918. Mrs Watkins of Eau Withington would also learn that her lance corporal son, a former farm labourer at Builth Farm, was dead. Old comrades also appealed for help. Soldier Dick Gibb contacted the *Hereford*

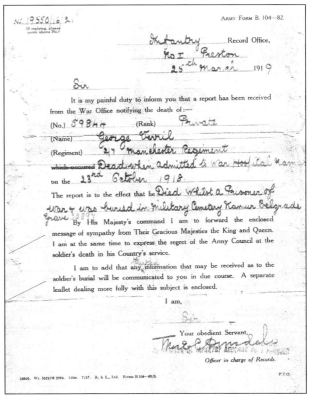

Munitioneer Kitty Verrill returned home to Peterchurch when the munitions works closed, but her parents, Alfred and Hannah, still had no news of her younger brother, 20-year-old George. It was months later that they found he had died as a prisoner of war. (Photo: Sue Verrill)

The Belgian refugees returned after the Armistice was declared leaving Irene Stewart, affectionately known as the Little Refugee, behind. The war had deprived the toddler of her family. Instead Irene was adopted by a kindly Malvern couple and went on to live a long and happy life. (Photo: Stuart Dove)

Released from Dartmoor Prison, conscientious objectors such as William Richardson returned home to Herefordshire. William, pictured with his son Norman, opened a small furniture shop in Widemarsh Street. (Photo: Norman Richardson)

Times desperate for any news of his friend Cpl George Lane from Ross, taken prisoner of war in 1918, while Gunner E.J. Tanswell wrote trying to find relatives of Cpl Jones and Pte Mason, killed and buried at Gallipoli. He had a photograph of their graves.

In April the National Kitchen closed and the last of the Belgians departed for home. Deputy Mayor Greenland, who had welcomed the refugees in the first place, congratulated them on having managed with the funds raised for them in 1914. They were, he said, a pleasure to work with. Some Belgians remained behind. One was the toddler Irene Stewart, affectionately known as the Little Refugee. She had arrived with her mother Charlotte and a Belgian family, the Verbecks, in 1915. After a spell in a house at 88 Bath Street, Irene had been placed in a Malvern hostel and Charlotte disappeared, ostensibly to find work. She was never seen again. Irene was brought up by a kindly Malvern family and went on to live a long and happy life.

As the Belgians departed, Herefordshire's prisoners of war were returning, among them Lt F. Gordon Challis from Hereford, Pte H.H. Grives from Ledbury, Pte W. Mytton from Kingsland and Pte C. Parsons from Ross. So too were the conscientious objectors. Harold Mostyn Watkins, the Ledbury teacher imprisoned for refusing to put on the King's uniform, was finally released from prison that year. The Gorsley builder Evan Watkins, sentenced to prison in 1916, was due for release in 1919. William Richardson, the Greenlands furniture salesman sentenced to hard labour at Wormwood Scrubs, had been found to have a 'genuine' case and been transferred from the Scrubs to Princetown Work Centre at Dartmoor Prison. The inmates stayed in unlocked cells, could wear civilian clothes rather than prison uniforms and could go out on Sundays. Richardson was released from Dartmoor in 1919, returning to Hereford where he took over and ran a small furniture store in Widemarsh Street. He was not formally discharged from the army, however, until March 1920.

Stanley Powell, the socialist tailor from Widemarsh Street, had gone missing. Having been sentenced to two years' hard labour by a North Wales court he had been imprisoned at Wormwood Scrubs, found 'genuine' when he appeared before a central tribunal in 1916 and placed on a work scheme, first at Talgarth and then Wakefield. But in 1918 Powell absconded from Wakefield. His father was hauled before Hereford magistrates and fined £10 for failing to help the police find him: he protested that he had last had contact with his son through the Manchester post office, but after that, nothing. Stanley Powell had disappeared.

Schools started assembling lists of former pupils killed in the war. Jim Thomas, a schoolboy at St Owens School in the 1930s, recalled the names of the dead being remembered in later years by a particularly stern headmaster, Mr W.W. Webber, who, on Armistice Day, 'stood there with this huge book and read off the names, the tears running down his face'. Hereford's Lord Scudamore School published its own list of 44 former children killed in the war, starting with Albert Ashurst and ending with George Yates.

Those still at school had problems of their own to contend with, especially over the issue of street football. This was beginning to be seen as a social problem and local authorities were urged to buy land to provide public football pitches.

The Education Committee meanwhile was endeavouring to deal with its own mismanagement after committee member G.F. Bulmer described the quality of education in Herefordshire as one of the worst in the country. The committee had received a report from the head of the Girls' High School, Miss Medwin, on the autumn 1918 examinations for 44 free places at her school. Only 4 had passed, she said, and not a single one of the 35 city and 9 country candidates had produced a good paper. Councillor Bulmer described her findings as an indictment of the county's elementary school system. One suggestion for improving standards was to set examinations for all 12-year-olds in school, but the committee rejected the plan for fear of introducing 'cramming' and because they feared elementary teachers would oppose it.

As for the children of the future, the Medical Officer for Health (Dr J.W. Miller was back in the job) reported that the birth rate, having caused alarm the previous year, was now 'exceptional', a fact which he attributed to the presence of so many munition workers. Dr Miller blamed influenza and slum housing as the main contributors to infant mortality, but pointed out that the death rate amongst illegitimate babies was almost twice that of babies born in wedlock.

St Francesca in Ledbury Road now served as the main home for unwed mothers. Situated on Ledbury Road close to its junction with Hafod Road, the home was registered under the name of the women's patrol leader Alice Butler and 52 births were registered there between 4 August 1918 and 5 March 1921. The unmarried mothers came from Hereford, Ross, Dilwyn, Yarkhill and Camberwell in London. There was no documentation to record the names of the fathers. Instead each birth was registered under the name of 'an informant', possibly a worker at the home: they included Blanche Redwood from Monmouth (she would emigrate to America in 1936), Dorothy Watts, Harriet Carlyon from Truro and Jessie Blower from Manchester.

The authorities had now begun to tackle almost five years of neglect in other areas. The Castle Green's public bowling green was reopened, although there were complaints that the rates, 3d per hour, were excessive. A review of the fire service equipment in Ledbury revealed serious shortcomings and a number of missing items including two ladders, a copper hand pump and a hose said to have been loaned to a local farmer and not returned.

The first phase of a £24,000 electrification scheme of the country districts around Hereford was announced, as was the resumption of shooting by the county's miniature rifle association. The May Fair went ahead despite a recommendation by Lady Butler that it be removed to a field near the city. (The former army recruitment tent was replaced with a temperance tent.) The Hunderton ferry was returned to service, the city council

Bodenham brothers William (front row, left) and Herbert Billings both returned home wounded by war: William lost the use of his right arm; Herbert had suffered shell shock. The two men worked as the village postmen until the 1950s. (Photo: Ivy Manning)

increasing ferryman Tom Edmunds' wages from 10 shillings to 15 shillings, while the Wye Board of Conservators, having permitted the netting of river fish, now announced the lowest catches ever recorded on the river. A total of 391 salmon and half a ton of coarse fish had been netted and sold to the public in 1918. However, poor conditions rather than over-fishing was blamed for the slump. The Conservators agreed that the bailiffs' jobs, held open for the duration of the war, were to be offered back to their loyal river men. Fifteen of the 16 bailiffs had enlisted in 1914: three had been killed in action, one was severely wounded, one had been gassed and another was too sick to return.

A more heartening story concerned the allotment movement and the quantity of vegetables grown during the war. The Ladies Horticultural Committee of Herefordshire had distributed £6,000 worth of vegetables during 1918 and the number of allotments in Hereford had risen from 147 before the war to 383 in April 1918, the land given over to allotments almost doubling to 32 acres. One allotment holder, however, noted that the city corporation was already serving notice on some plots now peace had been signed.

Walter Fuller returned home a hero having been awarded a Distinguished Conduct Medal. The Kington-born farm boy who had joined up at the age of 17 went on to become head gardener at Hennor Court. (Photo: Joyce Robins)

There was more good news from Miss Maddison of the HWWAC who announced that in May, seven new social clubs for country women had been set up. The new Women's Institutes, as they were to be called, had been founded at St Weonards, Brockhampton, Walford, Bishopswood, Garway, Goodrich, Brampton Bryan and Llanwarne.

Come Easter, when Reuben Davies arrived home on Good Friday having been demobbed after serving with the Worcester Regiment in Greece, he found no trains running and was left to walk the 13 miles home. The prospect of a narrow gauge railway assisting men such as Davies was slipping away, local leaders having decided that it would be expensive to run. As one put it: 'The future lies in motor traction.'

Herefordshire families were left to look forward with hope and backwards with sadness. How were the war dead to be remembered? Service medals and other honours were being distributed to men such as Walter James Fuller from Kington; the young soldier had been awarded the Distinguished Conduct Medal. Once out of uniform he slotted back into civilian life as a head gardener at Hennor Court near Leominster.

The county's first war memorial had been unveiled long before the war ended. In January

In October 1918 the new Order of the British Empire medals were awarded to Mrs Dorothy Kevill-Davies of Croft Castle and George Butcher, pictured in the centre surrounded by his workmates at Fryer's Garage. George had become the most famous ploughman in England. (Photo: Glen Butcher)

Brenda Lea was widowed in 1914 when her husband Captain Gerald Lea was killed. She wrote in her diary for 7 August 1919: 'Our wedding day. Have been married seven years.' She had noted Armistice Day the year before ('Great excitement. Flags decorating town. Public holiday') and on 11 November she cycled to the cathedral for the Armistice Day service: 'Two minutes silence at 11 '. Gardened in the afternoon'. (Herefordshire Records and Archive Centre)

The war dead of Cusop were added to the Hay on Wye memorial, unveiled in 1920.
It was placed in the town centre (and moved to a niche in the castle wall in 1957) after
discussions about siting it in the churchyard. One contributor suggested that some of the dead
would not have wanted a Christian symbol: the chair of the memorial committee, Lady Bailey
of Hay Castle, insisted that there had been no atheists amongst their fallen heroes.
(Photo: In Our Age)

1917 the dean led a ceremony at the Tupsley Cross. Dedicated by Lt Col Henry Hewat and his wife Jessie, the memorial listed the names of 32 men including their son Anthony, killed a month after the war began. Every year a single bunch of flowers and many poppy wreaths would be placed on the memorial steps.

In 1919 every parish looked at how to remember its dead, as a Colwall correspondent recommended that memorials be practical rather than ornamental and that all donations from 'shirkers or profiteers' be refused. Hereford City Council was still discussing where to site its memorial while Ross had formed a memorial committee and started fundraising. The Ross memorial was unveiled in 1921 at The Prospect looking out across the western hills of Herefordshire. It was built by Alfred Ursell of Waterloo House and carried the name of his son, 23-year-old Victor, killed in 1917.

Leominster decided on a swimming pool (the river-filled pool would be built in Lower Bridge Street) and a memorial tablet, Councillor W. St George Drennan calling the pool 'a memorial that would last as long as the town' and requesting a captured German gun to be placed in the town park. But the army council's offer of a war tank to Hereford prompted Councillor Wright to declare: 'Tanks are hideous, monstrous and terrible relics of the war. We cannot have a worse memorial.'

Kingsland considered a memorial hall after hearing they could secure a former YMCA war hut for around £500, but voted instead for a churchyard memorial. At Whitchurch, however, the generous offer of Mrs Katherine Levett to match every half-crown raised

In their efforts to remember the dead and provide funds for the necessary civic memorials in Hereford, a model of the Cenotaph was displayed in Hereford's High Town. (Photo: Herefordshire Libraries)

The tenant of Marsh Farm, Upton Bishop, Alfred James, who had been handed a white feather in Ross market, was wounded and sent home. After four years at war he found his family had been evicted from their home. (Photo: Keith James)

with 7s 6d of her own money saw the Whitchurch and Ganarew Memorial Hall built and opened by the Bishop of Hereford in 1923. As was the case in many village halls or churches, a brass plaque naming the village dead was set on one wall, in this instance listing Walter and Vivian Banchini and Harold, Wilfred and Leonard Redler, the five young men who had met outside the village post office back in 1913 (see page 1).

Six months after the war came to an end between 2,000 and 3,000 children gathered on Hereford's Castle Green to salute the flag for Empire Day. The colour party of the 1st Battalion Hereford Regiment had returned from Catterick Camp in Yorkshire having been halted in Leominster so that their arrival in Hereford could be marked with due ceremony and a reception that merited four columns of print in the *Hereford Times*.

The year had begun with a general election, but one ex-soldier, at least, turned his back on the celebrations and felt no desire to add his vote to the ballot box. After being handed a white feather at Ross market in 1915 Alfred James had left the home farm at Upton Bishop and joined the Royal Garrison Artillery. He had helped man the big guns in 1916 when, during the creeping barrage that was the prelude to the Battle of the Somme, he had slept little for seven days and nights. And 23 days before Germany signed for peace, he had been hit by gunshot, suffering a severe head wound. The Upton Bishop farmer's boy had been hospitalised and invalided out. The war over and his duty done, Alfred James returned home to find his family had been evicted from the farm because there was no man to work the land. James would never vote in an election again.

FURTHER READING
AND USEFUL SOURCES OF INFORMATION

The centenary of the First World War stimulated new research and inspired many innovative projects such as the Village Quire's performance of *Back to the Garden*, based on the letters of Corporal William Bevan (www.villagequire.org.uk), and the collaboration between young people at St Mary's School, Lugwardine and 2faced dance that celebrated the Croft family (www.trench.co.uk). In addition there have been tenacious individuals like Bill Webb (see below) whose memorial research in south Herefordshire revealed many new stories. There are many more stories to be told and the following should assist the reader with their research.

Herefordshire Libraries
www.herefordshire.gov.uk/libraries
The library service runs the Herefordshire History project (see below) and a local studies collection based at Hereford library (libraries@herefordshire.gov.uk).

Herefordshire History
www.herefordshirehistory.org.uk
The website carries a considerable amount of local history including wartime advertisements, illustrations, letters, diaries, stories, photographs and the digitised copies of all local newspapers from the period. The library welcomes new material that illustrates Herefordshire life (herefordshirehistory@herefordshire.gov.uk).

Herefordshire Museum Service
www.herefordshire.gov.uk/museums
The museum holds collections of First World War objects, photographs, posters, letters, ephemera, paintings and costumes available for study by appointment at the Museum Resource & Learning Centre, Friar Street, Hereford. There are also exhibition panels on Herefordshire in the Great War available for hire.

Herefordshire Archive and Records Centre (HARC)
www.herefordshire.gov.uk/archives
HARC holds a wide range of sources for local and family history in Herefordshire. From the records of the Hereford diocese and its parishes to the papers of landed estates,

courts and local government bodies, they help to tell the county's story and bring its past to life. The impact of the First World War is evident throughout the collection in letters, photographs, church registers and council minutes. They give a poignant account of tragedy and loss but also show how life continued outwardly unaffected by the conflict.

War memorials
www.herefordshire.gov.uk/wargraves
The Herefordshire war graves and war memorials list compiled by Jennifer Harrison gives information such as a dead soldier's home parish, the location of his memorial and brief family details.

Many local history groups have published their own memorial researches. The Garway war memorial book for example, researched by Joan Thomas of Garway Heritage Group (www.garwayheritagegroup.co.uk), lists the six who died out of the 41 who served in the war. Other local history groups have published specific works on the war from Leintwardine History Society's book, *Last Orders – Local Families on the Brink of War* (www.leintwardinehs.wordpress.com) to a group of historians in the Ewyas Harold district who published historical records relating to the war on their website: www.ewyaslacy.org.uk.

Some individuals have published their own research. Former librarian Bill Webb (billwebb.llangarron@gmail.com) compiled the stories of more than 170 soldiers from Ross parishes including Llangarron, Llangrove, Whitchurch, Ganarew, Walford, Goodrich, Sellack, Welsh Newton and parts of Ross itself. Copies of much of his work have been left in local churches.

Herefordshire Light Infantry Museum
www.herefordshirelightinfantrymuseum.com
The museum with its Hall of Honour and detailed history of the Herefordshire Light Infantry together with regimental photographs and artefacts is based at Suvla Barracks, Harold Street, Hereford, HR1 2QX.

Shropshire Regimental Museum
www.shropshireregimentalmuseum.co.uk
The museum at Shrewsbury Castle holds the history of the Kings Shropshire Light Infantry (KSLI). However the service and personal records that survive (most were destroyed during the Blitz) are based at the National Archives (www.nationalarchives. gov.uk) at Kew. A useful summary of the relevant KSLI papers at Kew is summarised on the Shropshire regimental museum website.

BBC
www.bbc.co.uk/herefordandworcester/ww1
Personal stories about the war from people who took part, and the impact it had on their families.

Herefordshire Lore
www.herefordshirelore.org.uk
More personal stories and local photographs published in the reminiscence project's quarterly journal, *In Our Age*. The material is searchable online.

Rotherwas Munitions Group
www.rotherwasmunitionshereford.co.uk
Over 12,000 worked at Rotherwas munitions factory during the two world wars and this group was formed in 2013 to collect the names of workers and commemorate their role. There are joint plans with the Skylon Enterprise Board to provide material for researchers and relatives at the Herefordshire Archive & Records Centre.

Herefordshire family history
www.herefordshirefhs.org.uk
With its surnames list and useful guidance on how to start researching family history, this is an important local resource.

Many of the county's independent museums (listed at www.herefordshire.gov.uk) hold information on Herefordshire in the First World War. They include Leominster Museum's Rifles and Spades project (www.leominstermuseum.org.uk) compiled by Deborah Jarman, which featured Leominster in the Great War.

Logaston Press
www.logastonpress.co.uk
Logaston Press continues to publish many books about Herefordshire and the central Marches. Books about the First World War include:

South Shropshire's First World War by Derek Beattie (2014)
ISBN 978 1 906663 82 7

The History of Rotherwas Munitions Factory, Hereford (2004) by John Edmonds
ISBN 978 1 904396 27 7

In the Munitions – Women at War in Herefordshire, ed Bill Laws (2003)
ISBN 978 1 873827 98 9

Other local books
Eardisland – An Oral History, Saxon Press (1995) ISBN 0 9526472 0 6
Herefordshire and World War One, published by the Workers' Educational Association (www.westmidlands.wea.org.uk)
Once They Lived in Gloucestershire by Linda Hart, Green Branch (2000) ISBN 0 9526031

General Index

Index of Places

Index of Names

Cooper, Alice (munitions) 115
  Pte Harry 50
  Henry Watkins (conscientious objector)
    65, 68
Corbett, Pte G.H. 52
Corbett-Winder, Mr *88*, 89
Corey, Violet 69
Corner, Alderman James 50, 84, 97, 122, 128
  Ellen Jane (munitions) 94
Cornewall, Sir Geoffrey 122
Cotterell, Lady Evelyn 47, 100, 123
  Sir John 22, 48, 55, 64-65, 84, 103, 110
Cotton, May 52
Cox, Leonard Stewart (conscientious objector)
    65
  Mabel Ann (munitions) 115
Craick, Dorothy 77
Crawshay, Miss Gertrude 28
Creasey, Clara 44
Cresswell, Herbert 125
Croft, Lady Ada 30, 40, 57
  Sir Herbert Archer 22, 28, 29, 30, 55-57
Croome, A.R. 112
Crump, George 122
Cullen, Maggie (munitions) 90
Cuming, Vice Admiral Robert 10
Curtis, Constable F.J. 87

Dalby, George 44
Dallow, Cpl Walter 98
Daly, Maurice 87
Davies, Sgt Charles 120
  L/Cpl Dick 32
  Dorothy 44
  Ethel 51
  Pte F. 99
  Fred 8
  George *14, 72*, 73
  George 122
  Griff 47
  Revd Herbert 66
  Ivor *14, 72*
  J. 117
  James *72*
  J.C. 113
  Joe (munitions) 115
  Signaller John 123
  Philip 61

Ralph Preece 18
R.E. 29
Roland 63
Thomas (conscientious objector) 125
W. 116
William 44
William (Fownhope) 62
W.J. 87
Dawson, A. Pudsey 123
Day, Lt Leslie 67
  Miss 74, 75
Deakin, S.H. 47
Deane, Evelyn (munitions) 115
Debenham, Colman 29
Decie, Col Prescott 31
  Miss 37, 100
Detheridge, A.J. 103
Dian, Jean 113
Dickinson, Mrs 52
Dixon, Pte William 78
Doorly, Revd M.E. 51
Dover, Miss (munitions) 115
Dowers, Charles 64
Downing, T. 25
Drage, Lt-Col 55, 99
Dredge, Allan 39
Drennan, W. St George 143
Dufty, Thomas 98-99
Duncan, Mr 84
Duncombe, L.M. 40
Dunnett, (munitions) 90
Dymond, Dorothy 31, 76, 81, 122
  councillor Edmund R. 26, 80, 91, 105,
    124, 126
Dyson, Gibson 48

Ecroyd, Miss 98
Edmunds, Pte Percy J. 99
Edwards, J. 135
  J. & R. (farmers) 61
  John and Margaret 124
  T. 63
Eldridge, Pte W. 54
Ellis, Pte Leonard 121
Elson, S.J. 45
Ely, Mrs 30
Emmott, Revd Theodore 97-98
Eskins, Ethel (munitions) 91

On the Trail of the Mortimers
With a Quiz and an I-Spy competition
by Philip Hume

This book both gives a history of the Mortimers (notably in their actions and impact on the central Marches) and includes a tour that explores the surviving physical remains that relate to the family. Partly through the good fortune of having an unbroken male succession for over 350 years, and also through conquest, marriage and royal favour, the Mortimers amassed a great empire of estates in England, Wales and Ireland; played key roles in the changing balance of power between the monarchy and nobles; deposed a king and virtually ruled the kingdom for three years; became, in later generations, close heirs to the throne through marriage; and seized the throne through battle when a Mortimer grandson became King Edward IV. A Quiz and an I-Spy have been designed to give pleasure to families wishing to find out more, with the successful completion of the latter leading to a certificate issued by the Mortimer History Society.

Paperback, 144 pages with over 75 colour photographs, maps and family trees   Price £7.50

Walking the Old Ways of Herefordshire:
the history in the landscape explored through 52 circular walks
by Andy and Karen Johnson

Each walk passes or visits a number of features about which some background information is given. These include churches, castle sites, deserted medieval villages, landscaping activity, quarrying, battle sites, dovecotes, hillforts, Iron Age farmsteads, Saxon dykes and ditches, individual farms and buildings, squatter settlements, almshouses, sculpture, burial sites, canals, disused railway lines – to name but a few, and including some that can only be reached on foot. The walks have also been chosen to help you explore Herefordshire from south to north, west to east, from quiet river valleys to airy hilltops, from ancient woodland to meadows and fields, from remote moorland to the historic streets of the county's towns, and of course Hereford itself. The walks range from 2½ to 9½ miles in length. The combination of photographs and historical information make this more than simply a book of walks, but also a companion to and celebration of Herefordshire.

Paperback, 384 pages, over 450 colour photographs and 53 maps   Price £12.95

Royalist, but ... Herefordshire in the English Civil War, 1640-51
by David Ross

On the eve of the Civil War in 1642, Herefordshire's leading families were all, to a greater or lesser extent, for the King – with the one notable exception of the Harleys at Brampton Bryan. As a result, Herefordshire was seen as a recruiting ground by Royalist military commanders, and as rather backward by some on the Parliamentary side. But once war had broken out with all its consequences, the majority were seen to be rather lukewarm in their support for the King. David Ross has a deep knowledge of this period which he uses with skill to craft a vivid picture of Herefordshire's inhabitants in these years of turmoil.

Paperback, 208 pages, 45 b/w illustrations   Price £12.95

Also from Logaston Press: www.logastonpress.co.uk

The Story of Hereford
Edited by Andy Johnson & Ron Shoesmith

This book tells the story of Hereford in breadth and depth, and includes the results of recent research and archaeological investigation. Alongside more familiar aspects of the city's history – how it fared in the Civil War, the foundation and history of the cathedral, the navigation of the Wye – there is new material on Saxon Hereford, medieval trade, Georgian Hereford and the activities of freehold land societies in the Victorian period. There is also information on less well known aspects of the city's past, including Hereford's prominence as a great centre of scientific and other learning at the end of the 12th century, and the use of the city as a base by Simon de Montfort, and also by Prince Henry in the wars with Owain Glyn Dwr. Whether you are familiar with Hereford's history or completely new to it, there is much here to interest, intrigue and surprise.

Paperback, 336 pages with over 160 colour and 50 mono illustrations   Price £15

The Parish that Disappeared; a History of St John's, Hereford
by Liz Pitman

From early in the 12th century until its final dissolution in 2012, the parish of St John's was at the heart of Hereford. Its houses and shops clustered around the cathedral, but it also encompassed land in Hereford. The relationship between the cathedral and the parish varied between amity and tension. But the history of the parish is as much the story of its characters, both the clergy who served it and the parishioners who lived within its bounds. There included paupers, old sailors, a comedian, actors, feltmakers, wool staplers, Italian apprentices and whores, whilst body snatchers also make an appearance.

Paperback, 128 pages with 30 colour and 30 mono illustrations   Price £10

The Archaeology of Herefordshire: An Exploration
by Keith Ray

Keith Ray was Herefordshire's County Archaeologist between 1998 and 2014, during which time he generated a wide range of exploratory projects, including many excavations. Much new knowledge and understanding of Herefordshire's archaeology has been gained as a result. In this study, he has described what is now known of the county's archaeology, assessing both the work of past generations and the discoveries of this modern era of enquiry. New insights are gained on the activities and rituals of our Neolithic ancestors, the ebb and flow of beliefs at the transition of the Neolithic into the Bronze Age, the shape of Saxon Hereford, the extent of an iron-working industry showing that Herefordshire was once a surprisingly industrial county, and much besides.

Paperback, 448 pages with 230 colour illustrations   Price £15